2 Grammar Connection

STRUCTURE THROUGH CONTENT

SERIES EDITORS

Marianne Celce-Murcia

M. E. Sokolik

Richard Firsten

THOMSON
HEINLE

Australia • Canada • Mexico • Singapore • United Kingdom • United States

THOMSON
™

HEINLE

Grammar Connection 2: Structure Through Content
Series Editors: Marianne Celce-Murcia, M. E. Sokolik
Richard Firsten

Publisher: *Sherrise Roehr*
Consulting Editor: *James W. Brown*
Director of Content Development:
  Anita Raducanu
Acquisitions Editor, Academic ESL:
  Tom Jefferies
Director of Product Marketing: *Amy Mabley*
Executive Marketing Manager: *Jim McDonough*
Senior Field Marketing Manager:
  Donna Lee Kennedy
Product Marketing Manager: *Katie Kelley*
Senior Development Editor: *Michael Ryall*
Assistant Editor: *Sarah Spader*
Editorial Assistant: *Katherine Reilly*

Cover Image: © Robert Harding World Imagery/
  Getty

Senior Production Project Manager:
  Maryellen Eschmann-Killeen
Manufacturing Buyer: *Betsy Donaghey*
Production Project Manager: *Chrystie Hopkins*
Production Services:
  InContext Publishing Partners
Index: *Alexandra Nickerson*
Cover and Interior Designer: *Linda Beaupre*
Printer: *Courier Kendallville*

Printed in the United States of America.
1 2 3 4 5 6 7 8 9 10 — 11 10 09 08 07

For more information contact Thomson Heinle,
25 Thomson Place, Boston, Massachusetts
02210 USA, or you can visit our Internet site at
http://elt.thomson.com

Credits appear on pages 265–267, which
constitutes a continuation of the copyright page.

ISBN 10: 1-4130-0835-6
ISBN 13: 978-1-4130-0835-7

International Student Edition
ISBN 10: 1-4130-1752-5
ISBN 13: 978-1-4130-1752-6

Library of Congress Control Number:
2006909604

Contents

 Using language grammatically and being able to communicate authentically are important goals for students. My grammar research suggests that students' mastery of grammar improves when they interpret and produce grammar in meaningful contexts at the discourse level. *Grammar Connection* connects learners to academic success, allowing them to reach their goals and master the grammar.

— Marianne Celce-Murcia

 "Connections" is probably the most useful concept in any instructor's vocabulary. To help students connect what they are learning to the rest of their lives is the most important task I fulfill as an instructor. *Grammar Connection* lets instructors and students find those connections. The series connects grammar to reading, writing, and speaking. It also connects students with the ability to function academically, to use the Internet for interesting research, and to collaborate with others on projects and presentations. — M. E. Sokolik

Dear Instructor,

With experience in language teaching, teacher training, and research, we created *Grammar Connection* to be uniquely relevant for academically and professionally oriented courses and students. Every lesson in the series deals with academic content to help students become familiar with the language of college and the university and to feel more comfortable in all of their courses, not just English.

While academic content provides the context for this series, our goal is for the learner to go well beyond sentence-level exercises in order to use grammar as a resource for comprehending and producing academic discourse. Students move from shorter, more controlled exercises to longer, more self-directed, authentic ones. Taking a multi-skills approach, *Grammar Connection* includes essential grammar that students need to know at each level. Concise lessons allow instructors to use the material easily in any classroom situation.

We hope that you and your students find our approach to the teaching and learning of grammar for academic and professional purposes in *Grammar Connection* effective and innovative.

Marianne Celce-Murcia
Series Editor

M. E. Sokolik
Series Editor

■ What is *Grammar Connection*?

Grammar Connection is a five-level grammar series that integrates content with grammar instruction in an engaging format to prepare students for future academic and professional success.

■ What is the content?

The content in *Grammar Connection* is drawn from various academic disciplines: sociology, psychology, medical sciences, computer science, communications, biology, engineering, business, and the social sciences.

■ Why does *Grammar Connection* incorporate content into the lessons?

The content is used to provide high-interest contexts for exploring the grammar. The charts and exercises are contextualized with the content in each lesson. Learning content is not the focus of *Grammar Connection*—it sets the scene for learning grammar.

■ Is *Grammar Connection* "discourse-based"?

Yes. With *Grammar Connection,* learners go beyond sentence-level exercises in order to use grammar as a resource for comprehending and producing academic discourse. These discourses include conversations, narratives, and exposition.

■ Does *Grammar Connection* include communicative practice?

Yes. *Grammar Connection* takes a multi-skills approach. The series includes listening activities as well as texts for reading, and the production tasks elicit both spoken and written output via pair or group work tasks.

■ Why are the lessons shorter than in other books?

Concise lessons allow instructors to use the material easily in any classroom situation. For example, one part of a lesson could be covered in a 50-minute period, allowing instructors with shorter class times to feel a sense of completion. Alternatively, a single lesson could fit into a longer, multi-skills class period. For longer, grammar-focused classes, more than one lesson could be covered.

■ Does *Grammar Connection* include opportunities for students to review the grammar?

Yes. A Review section is included after every five lessons. These tests can also be used by instructors to measure student understanding of the grammar taught. In addition, there are practice exercises in the Workbook and on the website (elt.thomson.com/grammarconnection).

■ Does *Grammar Connection* assist students in learning new vocabulary?

Yes. The Content Vocabulary section in each lesson of *Grammar Connection* incorporates academic vocabulary building and journaling. In Book 1 this takes a picture dictionary approach. In later books words from the Academic Word List are used. This, along with the content focus, ensures that students expand their vocabulary along with their grammatical capability.

Grammar Connection is organized into thirty concise lessons, each containing two or three parts of connected grammar points. Every lesson follows a unique pedagogical approach.

A **picture-based vocabulary** section in lower levels familiarizes students with the content-based academic vocabulary that is used in the lesson. At higher levels, students are introduced to words from the **Academic Word List.**

The grammar in each lesson is **contextualized** with topics from different **academic disciplines.**

Thought-provoking **discussion questions** activate students' knowledge of the content area. The questions can also be used as **diagnostic tests** to assess students' mastery of the grammar before it is taught.

An integrated **audio program** allows students to listen to the content readings and dialogues.

Content readings and dialogues present the grammar in a meaningful and interesting way.

Contextualized grammar charts provide **easy-to-understand** clear explanations of grammar form as well as notes on usage.

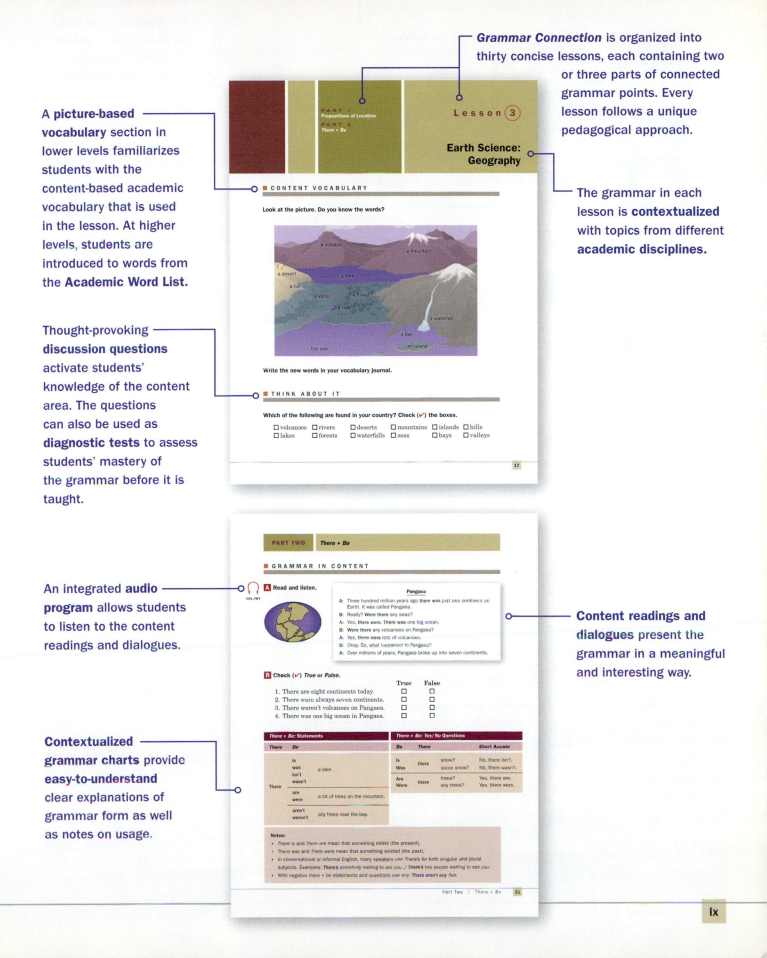

PART 1
Prepositions of Location
PART 2
There + Be

Lesson ③

Earth Science: Geography

■ CONTENT VOCABULARY

Look at the picture. Do you know the words?

a volcano   a mountain
a desert   a lake
a hill   a valley   a forest
a river   a waterfall
a bay
the sea   an island

Write the new words in your vocabulary journal.

■ THINK ABOUT IT

Which of the following are found in your country? Check (✔) the boxes.

☐ volcanoes ☐ rivers ☐ deserts ☐ mountains ☐ islands ☐ hills
☐ lakes ☐ forests ☐ waterfalls ☐ seas ☐ bays ☐ valleys

17

PART TWO   *There + Be*

■ GRAMMAR IN CONTENT

A Read and listen.

CD1,TR7

Pangaea

A: Three hundred million years ago there was just one continent on Earth. It was called Pangaea.
B: Really? Were there any seas?
A: Yes, there were. There was one big ocean.
B: Were there any volcanoes on Pangaea?
A: Yes, there were lots of volcanoes.
B: Okay. So, what happened to Pangaea?
A: Over millions of years, Pangaea broke up into seven continents.

B Check (✔) *True* or *False*.

	True	False
1. There are eight continents today.	☐	☐
2. There were always seven continents.	☐	☐
3. There weren't volcanoes on Pangaea.	☐	☐
4. There was one big ocean in Pangaea.	☐	☐

There + Be: Statements

There	Be	
There	is was isn't wasn't	a lake.
	are were	a lot of trees on the mountain.
	aren't weren't	any trees near the bay.

There + Be: Yes/No Questions

Be	There		Short Answer
Is Was	there	snow? some snow?	No, there isn't. No, there wasn't.
Are Were	there	trees? any trees?	Yes, there are. Yes, there were.

Notes:
• *There is* and *There are* mean that something exists (the present).
• *There was* and *There were* mean that something existed (the past).
• In conversational or informal English, many speakers use *There's* for both singular and plural subjects. Examples: *There's somebody waiting to see you. / There's two people waiting to see you.*
• With negative *there + be* statements and questions use *any*: *There aren't any fish.*

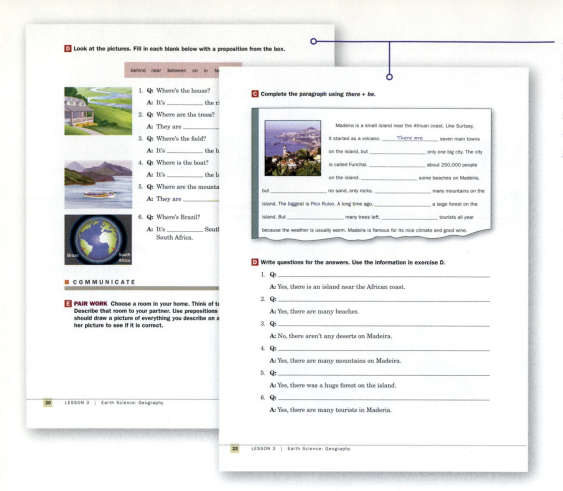

D Look at the pictures. Fill in each blank below with a preposition from the box.

behind near between on in fa...

1. **Q:** Where's the house?
   A: It's _____ the ri...
2. **Q:** Where are the trees?
   A: They are _____
3. **Q:** Where's the field?
   A: It's _____ the h...
4. **Q:** Where is the boat?
   A: It's _____ the la...
5. **Q:** Where are the mounta...
   A: They are _____
6. **Q:** Where's Brazil?
   A: It's _____ Sout...
   South Africa.

Brazil South Africa

■ COMMUNICATE

E **PAIR WORK** Choose a room in your home. Think of te...
Describe that room to your partner. Use prepositions ...
should draw a picture of everything you describe on a...
her picture to see if it is correct.

C Complete the paragraph using *there + be*.

Madeira is a small island near the African coast. Like Surtsey, it started as a volcano. _There are_ seven main towns on the island, but _____ only one big city. The city is called Funchal. _____ about 250,000 people on the island. _____ some beaches on Madeira, but _____ no sand, only rocks. _____ many mountains on the island. The biggest is Pico Ruivo. A long time ago, _____ a large forest on the island. But _____ many trees left. _____ tourists all year because the weather is usually warm. Madeira is famous for its nice climate and good wine.

D Write questions for the answers. Use the information in exercise D.

1. **Q:** _____
   A: Yes, there is an island near the African coast.
2. **Q:** _____
   A: Yes, there are many beaches.
3. **Q:** _____
   A: No, there aren't any deserts on Madeira.
4. **Q:** _____
   A: Yes, there are many mountains on Madeira.
5. **Q:** _____
   A: Yes, there was a huge forest on the island.
6. **Q:** _____
   A: Yes, there are many tourists in Maderia.

Students move from a **variety** of controlled exercises to more self-directed ones enabling students to become comfortable using the grammar.

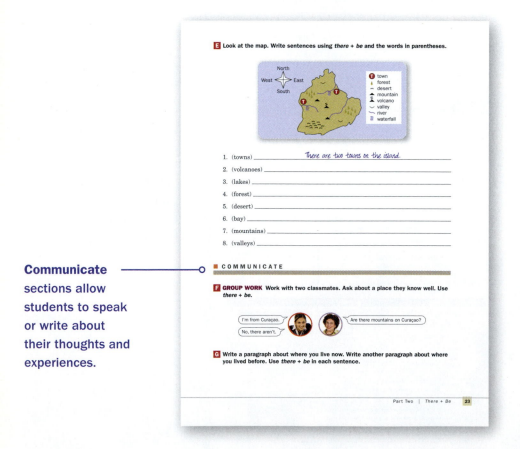

E Look at the map. Write sentences using *there + be* and the words in parentheses.

North
West ◆ East
South

T town
↑ forest
≈ desert
▲ mountain
△ volcano
∨ valley
~ river
▤ waterfall

1. (towns) _____ There are two towns on the island. _____
2. (volcanoes) _____
3. (lakes) _____
4. (forest) _____
5. (desert) _____
6. (bay) _____
7. (mountains) _____
8. (valleys) _____

■ COMMUNICATE

F **GROUP WORK** Work with two classmates. Ask about a place they know well. Use *there + be*.

I'm from Curaçao.
No, there aren't.

Are there mountains on Curaçao?

G Write a paragraph about where you live now. Write another paragraph about where you lived before. Use *there + be* in each sentence.

Communicate sections allow students to speak or write about their thoughts and experiences.

At the end of each lesson, students are encouraged to put together the **grammar and vocabulary** from the lesson in a productive way.

Interesting projects allow students to put newly learned grammatical forms and vocabulary to use in ways that encourage additional independent reading, **research,** and/or communication. Many of these activities are group activities, further requiring students to put their language skills to work.

Internet activities encourage students to connect the grammar with online resources.

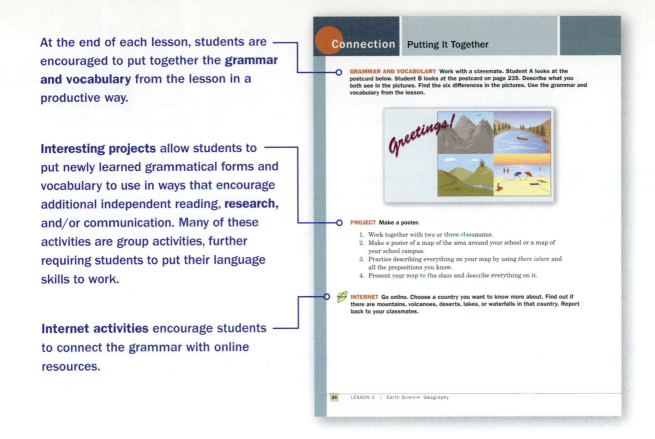

Connection   Putting It Together

GRAMMAR AND VOCABULARY Work with a classmate. Student A looks at the postcard below. Student B looks at the postcard on page 235. Describe what you both see in the pictures. Find the six differences in the pictures. Use the grammar and vocabulary from the lesson.

PROJECT Make a poster.

1. Work together with two or three classmates.
2. Make a poster of a map of the area around your school or a map of your school campus.
3. Practice describing everything on your map by using *there is/are* and all the prepositions you know.
4. Present your map to the class and describe everything on it.

INTERNET Go online. Choose a country you want to know more about. Find out if there are mountains, volcanoes, deserts, lakes, or waterfalls in that country. Report back to your classmates.

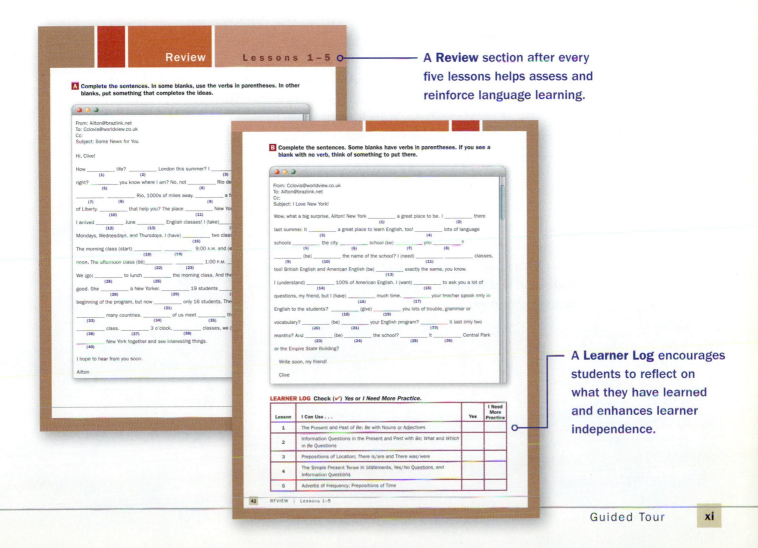

Review   Lessons 1–5

A **Review** section after every five lessons helps assess and reinforce language learning.

A Complete the sentences. In some blanks, use the verbs in parentheses. In other blanks, put something that completes the ideas.

From: Ailton@brazlink.net
To: Cclovis@worldview.co.uk
Cc:
Subject: Some News for You

Hi, Clive!

How _____ life? _____ London this summer? I _____
            (1)   (2)   (3)
right? _____ you know where I am? No, not _____ Rio de
          (5)   (6)
_____ _____ Rio, 1000s of miles away. _____ a fa
     (7)   (8)   (9)
of Liberty. _____ that help you? The place _____ New Yor
                      (10)   (11)
I arrived _____ June _____ English classes! I (take)_____
               (12)   (13)
Mondays, Wednesdays, and Thursdays. I (have) _____ two class
                                                                   (16)
The morning class (start) _____ _____ 9:00 A.M. and (e
                                  (18)   (19)
noon. The afternoon class (be)_____ _____ 1:00 P.M. _____
                                          (22)   (23)
We (go) _____ to lunch _____ the morning class. And the
             (25)   (26)
good. She _____ a New Yorker. _____ 19 students _____
                (28)   (29)
beginning of the program, but now _____ only 16 students. The
                                              (31)
_____ many countries. _____ of us meet _____ th
   (33)   (34)   (35)
_____ class. _____ 3 o'clock, _____ classes, we (
   (36)   (37)   (38)
_____ New York together and see interesting things.
   (40)

I hope to hear from you soon.

Ailton

B Complete the sentences. Some blanks have verbs in parentheses. If you see a blank with no verb, think of something to put there.

From: Cclovis@worldview.co.uk
To: Ailton@brazlink.net
Cc:
Subject: I Love New York!

Wow, what a big surprise, Ailton! New York _____ a great place to be. I _____ there
                                                          (1)   (2)
last summer. It _____ a great place to learn English, too! _____ lots of language
                       (3)   (4)
schools _____ the city. _____ school (be) _____ you _____?
              (5)   (6)   (7)   (8)
_____ (be) _____ the name of the school? I (need) _____ _____ classes,
   (9)   (10)   (11)
too! British English and American English (be) _____ exactly the same, you know.
                                                        (13)
I (understand) _____ 100% of American English. I (want) _____ to ask you a lot of
                    (14)   (15)
questions, my friend, but I (have) _____ much time. _____ your teacher speak only in
                                        (16)   (17)
English to the students? _____ (give) _____ you lots of trouble, grammar or
                                  (18)   (19)
vocabulary? _____ (be) _____ your English program? _____ It last only two
                  (20)   (21)   (22)
months? And _____ (be) _____ the school? _____ it _____ Central Park
                   (23)   (24)   (25)   (26)
or the Empire State Building?

Write soon, my friend!

Clive

A **Learner Log** encourages students to reflect on what they have learned and enhances learner independence.

LEARNER LOG Check (✓) *Yes* or *I Need More Practice.*

Lesson	I Can Use . . .	Yes	I Need More Practice
1	The Present and Past of *Be*; *Be* with Nouns or Adjectives		
2	Information Questions in the Present and Past with *Be*; *What* and *Which* in *Be* Questions		
3	Prepositions of Location; *There is/are* and *There was/were*		
4	The Simple Present Tense in Statements, Yes/No Questions, and Information Questions		
5	Adverbs of Frequency; Prepositions of Time		

■ Audio Program

Audio CDs and Audio Tapes allow students to listen to every reading in the book to build listening skills and fluency.

■ Workbook

The workbooks review and practice all the grammar points in the Student Book. In addition each workbook includes six Writing Tutorials and vocabulary expansion exercises.

■ Website

Features additional grammar practice activities, vocabulary test items, and other resources: elt.thomson.com/ grammarconnection.

■ Annotated Teacher's Edition with Presentation Tool CD-ROM

Offers comprehensive lesson planning advice and teaching tips, as well as a full answer key. The Presentation Tool CD-ROM includes a PowerPoint presentation for selected lessons and includes all the grammar charts from the book.

■ Assessment CD-ROM with ExamView® Pro Test Generator

The customizable generator features lesson, review, mid-term, and term-end assessment items to monitor student progress.

Grammar Connection is based on scientific research on the most effective means of teaching grammar to adult learners of English.

■ Discourse-based Grammar

Research by Celce-Murcia and Olshtain (2000) suggests that learners should go beyond sentence-level exercises in order to use grammar as a resource for comprehending and producing academic discourse. *Grammar Connection* lets students move from controlled exercises to more self-expressive and self-directed ones.

■ Communicative Grammar

Research shows that communicative exercises should complement traditional exercises (Comeau, 1987; Herschensohn, 1988). *Grammar Connection* balances effective controlled activities, such as fill-in-the-blanks, with meaningful interactive exercises.

■ Learner-centered Content

Van Duzer (1999) emphasizes that research on adult English language learners shows that "learners should read texts that meet their needs and are interesting." In *Grammar Connection* the content readings are carefully selected and adapted to be both high-interest and relevant to the needs of learners.

■ Vocabulary Development

A number of recent studies have shown the effectiveness of helping English language learners develop independent skills in vocabulary development (Nation, 1990, 2001; Nist & Simpson, 2001; Schmitt, 2000). In *Grammar Connection,* care has been taken to introduce useful academic vocabulary, based in part on Coxhead's (2000) work.

■ Using Background Knowledge

Because research shows that background knowledge facilitates comprehension (Eskey, 1997), each lesson of *Grammar Connection* opens with a "Think About It" section related to the lesson theme.

■ Student Interaction

Learning is enhanced when students work with each other to co-construct knowledge (Grennon-Brooks & Brooks, 1993; Sutherland & Bonwell, 1996). *Grammar Connection* includes many pair and group work exercises as well as interactive projects.

■ References

Celce-Murcia, M., & Olshtain, E. (2000). *Discourse and Context in Language Teaching.* New York: Cambridge University Press.

Comeau, R. Interactive Oral Grammar Exercises. In W. M. Rivers (Ed.), *Interactive Language Teaching* (57–69). Cambridge: Cambridge University Press, 1987.

Coxhead, A. (2000). "A New Academic Word List." *TESOL Quarterly,* 34 (2), 213–238.

Eskey, D. (1997). "Models of Reading and the ESOL Student." *Focus on Basics 1 (B),* 9–11.

Grennon Brooks, J., & Brooks, M. G. (1993). *In Search of Understanding: The Case for Constructivist Classrooms.* Alexandria, VA: Association for Supervision and Curriculum Development.

Herschensohn, J. (1988). "Linguistic Accuracy of Textbook Grammar." *Modern Language Journal 72(4),* 409–414.

Nation, I. S. P. (2001). *Learning Vocabulary in Another Language.* New York: Cambridge University Press.

Nation, I. S. P. (1990). *Teaching and Learning Vocabulary.* Boston: Thomson Heinle.

Nist, S. L., & Simpson, M. L. (2001). *Developing Vocabulary for College Thinking.* Boston: Allyn & Bacon.

Schmitt, N. (2000). *Vocabulary in Language Teaching.* New York: Cambridge University Press.

Sutherland, T. E., & Bonwell, C. C. (Eds.). (1996). "Using Active Learning in College Classes: A Range of Options for Faculty." *New Directions for Teaching and Learning, Number 67,* Fall 1996. San Francisco, CA: Jossey-Bass Publishers.

VanDuzer, C. (1999). "Reading and the Adult Language Learner." *ERIC Digest.* Washington, D.C.: National Center for ESL Literacy Education.

I owe a debt of gratitude to all the students I have had over the years and all my colleagues I have worked with over the years. They have been responsible for teaching me my craft.

I would like to thank Bruce Fontaine, whose support and understanding greatly helped me meet the challenge of writing this book.

— Richard Firsten

The author, series editors, and publisher wish to thank the following people for their contributions:

Susan Alexandre
Trimble Technical High School
Fort Worth, TX

Joan Amore
Triton College
River Grove, IL

Cally Andriotis-Williams
Newcomers High School
Long Island City, NY

Ana Maria Cepero
Miami Dade College
Miami, FL

Jacqueline Cunningham
Harold Washington College
Chicago, IL

Kathleen Flynn
Glendale Community College
Glendale, CA

Sally Gearhart
Santa Rosa Junior College
Santa Rosa, CA

Janet Harclerode
Santa Monica College
Santa Monica, CA

Carolyn Ho
North Harris College
Houston, TX

Eugenia Krimmel
Lititz, PA

Dana Liebowitz
Palm Beach Central High
    School
Wellington, FL

Shirley Lundblade
Mt. San Antonio College
Walnut, CA

Craig Machado
Norwalk Community College
Norwalk, CT

Myo Myint
Mission College
Santa Clara, CA

Myra Redman
Miami Dade College
Miami, FL

Eric Rosenbaum
BEGIN Managed Programs
New York, NY

Marilyn Santos
Valencia Community College
Valencia, FL

Laura Sicola
University of Pennsylvania
Philadelphia, PA

Barbara Smith-Palinkas
University of South Florida
Tampa, FL

Kathy Sucher
Santa Monica College
Santa Monica, CA

Patricia Turner
San Diego City College
San Diego, CA

America Vasquez
Miami Dade College, Inter-
    American Campus
Miami, FL

Tracy von Mulaski
El Paso Community College
El Paso, TX

Jane Wang
Mt. San Antonio College
Walnut, CA

Lucy Watel
City College of Chicago - Harry
    S. Truman College
Chicago, IL

Donald Weasenforth
Collin County Community
    College
Plano, TX

Pre-Lesson

Orientation

PART ONE	Classroom Instructions

read

ask   answer

> What's your name?
>
> My name is Kaito.

discuss

> I think that . . .
>
> I think . . .

listen

Instruction	Example
Underline the adjective.	I have a <u>new</u> dictionary.
Circle the verb.	You (work) in a school.
Fill in the blank.	She ___is___ a teacher.
Complete the sentence.	I speak ___Spanish and English.___
Match the items.	1. _b_ noun a. new 2. _a_ adjective b. book
Correct the sentence.	I is a student. ^am
Choose the correct answer.	They (is / (are)) my friends.
Check (✔) the correct answer.	English is a country. ___ English is a language. ✔
Put the words in order.	from are We China. ___We are from China.___
Write a sentence.	_I am a student._
Write a paragraph.	_I am a student. I study history. One day I want to be a history professor at a university._

A **Match the items.**

1. _b_ listen   a. noun

2. ___ instructor   b. verb

3. ___ small   c. pronoun

4. ___ she   d. adjective

B **Underline the nouns.**

<u>a clock</u>   listen   white   a teacher   happy   run   a backpack

C (Circle) **the verbs.**

(read)   a book   a house   eat   old   talk   expensive

D **Check (✔) the correct answers.**

1. "a cat" is: ✔ a noun   ___ a verb

2. "eat" is: ___ a noun   ___ a verb

3. "happy" is: ___ a verb   ___ an adjective

4. "they" is: ___ an adjective   ___ a pronoun

E **Correct the sentences.**

1. "An instructor" is a ~~verb~~.   3. "It" is an adjective.

2. "Eat" is a noun.   *noun*   4. "Happy" is a pronoun.

PART TWO	Vocabulary Journal

In this textbook you will learn a lot of new vocabulary. Use a vocabulary journal to help you learn these new words. To create a vocabulary journal you should:

1. Write a letter of the alphabet at the top of each page.
2. Write new words in your vocabulary journal under the correct letter.
3. Draw a picture or write a definition and a sentence using each word.
4. Study the words every evening.

PART 1
The Present and Past of *Be*

PART 2
Be + Nouns or Adjectives

Lesson 1

Physical Science: Meteorology

CONTENT VOCABULARY

Look at the pictures. Do you know the words?

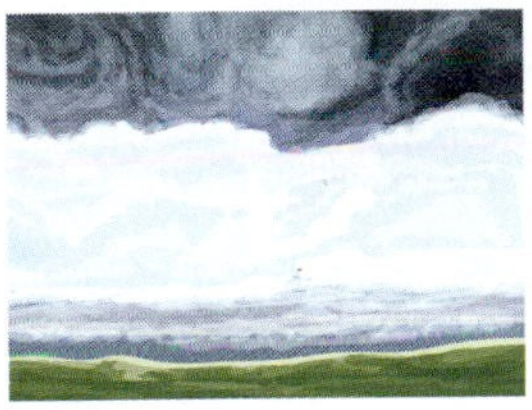
cloudy

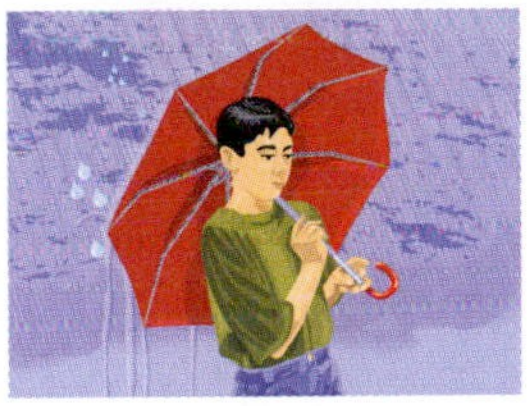
rainy

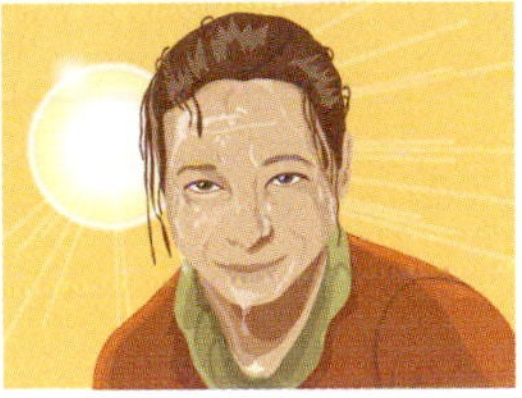
humid

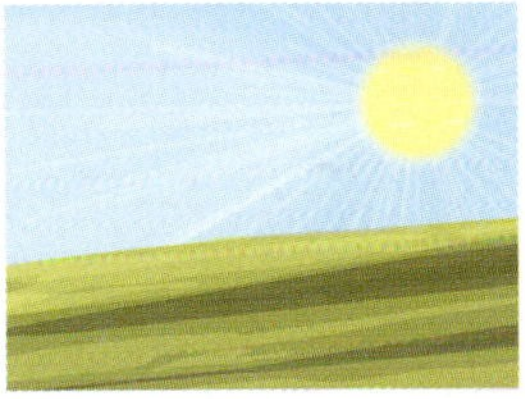
sunny

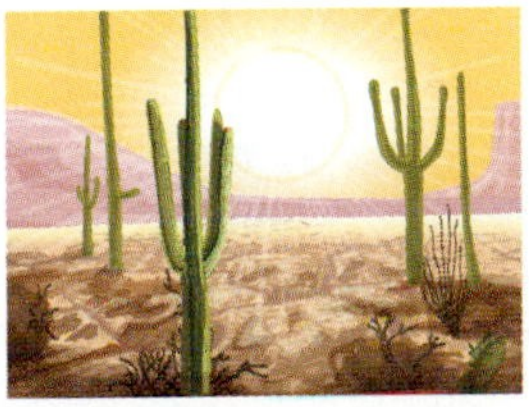
dry

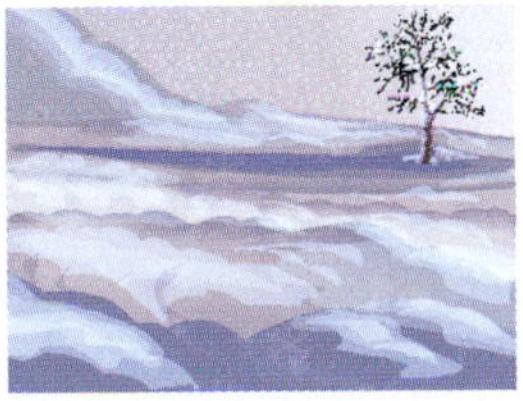
snowy

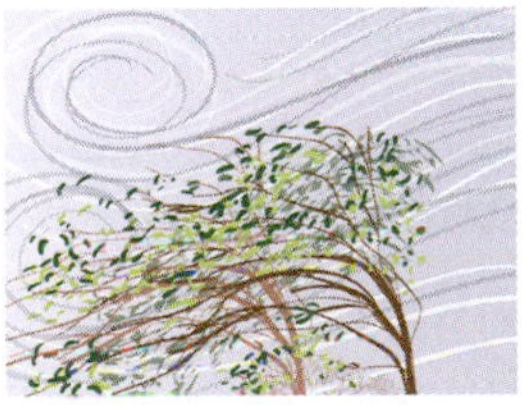
windy

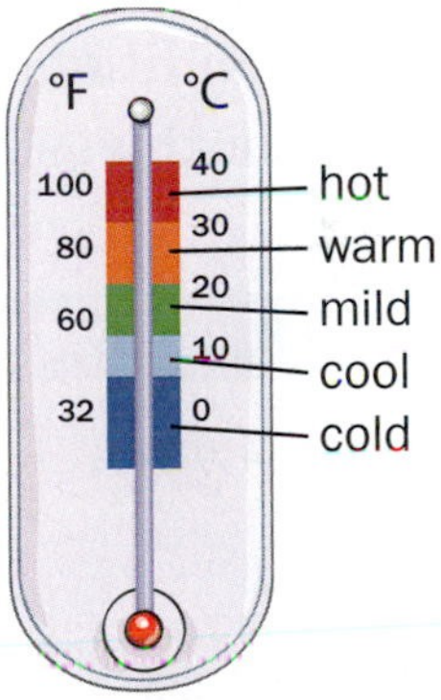

°F
°C
100
80
60
32
40
30
20
10
0
hot
warm
mild
cool
cold

Write the new words in your vocabulary journal.

THINK ABOUT IT

What's the weather like today? What was it like yesterday? Discuss these questions in groups.

■ GRAMMAR IN CONTENT

A **Read and listen.**

CD1,TR1

Weather and Climate

Meteorology **is** the study of weather and climate. Weather **is** the condition of the sky and air each day. Maybe yesterday it **was** sunny. Today conditions **are not** the same. It**'s** cloudy. How **was** the weather yesterday? How **is** it today?

Climate **is** the weather for a long period of time. The climate in the northwestern United States **is** very different from the southwestern United States. Northwestern states **are** often rainy for most of the year. Southwestern states **aren't** rainy. It**'s** usually dry there all year. Conditions **were** different millions of years ago. Climate changes very slowly.

condition: state of something   **same:** alike, equal   **different:** not alike, unequal

B **Check (✔) _True_ or _False_.**

	True	False
1. Meteorology is the study of weather and climate.	☐	☐
2. Northwestern states are often rainy.	☐	☐
3. Conditions were the same millions of years ago.	☐	☐
4. Southwestern states are very dry for half of the year.	☐	☐

The Present and Past of _Be:_ Statements

Subject	_Be_		Subject	_Be_	
I	am am not	a teacher.	I	was was not	a doctor.
He She It	is is not	warm.	He She It	was was not	warm yesterday.
We You They	are are not	Mexicans.	We You They	were were not	in Mexico last year.

Notes:

- Use *be* to talk about people, places, and things.
- Use *it* and *be* to talk about weather. Example: *It is cloudy.*
- The contractions for the present of *be*: *I'm, He's, She's, You're, We're,* and *They're*
- The contractions for the negative of *be*: *I'm not, He's not, He isn't, She's not, She isn't, You're not, You aren't, We're not, We aren't, They're not, They aren't*
- There are no contractions with *was* and *were* in affirmative statements (~~I's, we're~~).
- Some past time expressions are **yesterday; last week / month / year; one week / two months / four years ago.**
- Use contractions in informal speech and informal writing.

The Present and Past of *Be*: *Yes/No* Questions

Present *Yes/No* Questions and Short Answers with *Be*		Past *Yes/No* Questions and Short Answers with *Be*	
Yes/No Question	**Short Answer**	**Yes/No Question**	**Short Answer**
Am I cold?	Yes, **you are.** No, **you're not.** No, **you aren't.**	Was I cold?	Yes, **you were.** No, **you were not.** No, **you weren't.**
Is he/she/it cold?	Yes, **he/she/it is.** No, **he/she/it is not.** No, **he/she/it isn't.** No, **he's/she's/it's not.**	Was he/she/it cold?	Yes, **he/she/it was.** No, **he/she/it was not.** No, **he/she/it wasn't.**
Are we cold?	Yes, **we are.** No, **we're not.** No, **we aren't.**	Were we cold?	Yes, **we were.** No, **we were not.** No, **we weren't.**

Notes:

- We use negative questions when we think we know the answer. Example: *Isn't it hot in here?* (The speaker thinks the listener will say, *Yes, it is.*)
- The negative question for *I am* is *Aren't I?* Example: *Aren't I in the Level 2 class?*

C **Write questions using the words. Then, write answers that are true for you.**

1. you / are / a student

   Q: _____ Are you a student? _____

   A: _____ Yes, I am. I am a student. _____

2. you / last year / were / a student

   Q: _____

   A: _____

3. your class / is / in the United States

   Q: _____

   A: _____

4. is / sunny today / it

   Q: _____

   A: _____

5. it / snowy yesterday / was

   Q: _____

   A: _____

D **Complete the dialogue with a form of *be*.**

Bob: Hi. _____*Are you*_____ Amir?
(1)

Amir: Yes, _____. _____ my new roommate?
(2)   (3)

Bob: No, _____. My name _____ Bob.
(4)   (5)

_____ a new student?
(6)

Amir: Yes, that _____ right. I _____ from Libya. It
(7)   (8)

_____ a country in North Africa.
(9)

Bob: I know. Hmm . . . _____ Libya very hot all the time?
(10)

Amir: No, it _____. But it _____ hot there right
(11)   (12)

now because it _____ August.
(13)

Bob: I _____ in Egypt last year in December. It
(14)

_____ hot then. I needed a sweater.
(15)

I _____ surprised.
(16)

Amir: In North Africa the weather _____ sometimes hot and
(17)

sometimes cold, but it _____ always very dry.
(18)

Bob: Well, not here. The climate here _____ dry. Many
(19)

days of the year _____ rainy. The past two years
(20)

_____ very rainy. Our climate and Libya's climate
(21)

_____ very different.
(22)

Amir: Yes, they _____.
(23)

E Look at the chart. Write sentences about the climate in each city using *be.*

Climate for Selected Cities					
City	June	December	City	June	December
Buenos Aires	mild	warm, wet	Moscow	hot, dry	very cold, snowy
Cairo	very hot, dry	mild, dry	New York	hot, sunny	cold
Johannesburg	cool, dry	warm, rainy	Singapore	hot, humid	hot, humid, rainy

1. _In Buenos Aires, it is mild in June and warm and wet in December._

2. _____

3. _____

4. _____

5. _____

6. _____

F Complete the sentences with true statements about the weather. Use *be* in the past.

1. _____ yesterday.

2. _____ two days ago.

3. _____ last week.

■ **C O M M U N I C A T E**

G **PAIR WORK** Use each word in the box to make a question. Work with a classmate. Ask a question. Your classmate will give the answer. Take turns.

sunny	50 degrees	tornadoes	hot	dangerous
yesterday	droughts	scientist	cloudy	storm

Is it sunny today?   Yes, it is.

H WRITE Write about the weather and climate in a country you know well.

> I am Pilar. I'm from Lima, Peru. It rains in Lima in July, August, and September. It is usually dry most of the year. The temperatures are warm in January but cool in July.

PART TWO	*Be* + Nouns or Adjectives

■ **GRAMMAR IN CONTENT**

CD1,TR2

A Read and listen.

tornado

Dangerous Weather

Tornadoes **are rare**. They don't happen very often. But when they happen, tornadoes **are** very **dangerous**.

Tornadoes **are strong** storms. Most tornadoes have winds of 110 mph and are 250 feet across. It **is** very **dangerous** in the American Midwest in the spring. For example, in 1974 there were over 140 tornadoes in 13 states in one day. One tornado destroyed part of a city in Ohio. The storms **were quick** and **powerful**. It **was** very **windy**. People **were** very **scared**. Over 300 people died.

dangerous: harmful   **mph:** miles per hour

B Read the passage again. (Circle) **the best answers.**

1. Tornadoes are   a. pretty.   b. nice.   c. dangerous.
2. Tornadoes are   a. scared.   b. slow.   c. rare.
3. The storms of 1974 were   a. small.   b. deadly.   c. slow.
4. People were   a. scared.   b. dangerous.   c. powerful.

Noun + *Be* + Adjective	*Be* + Adjective + Noun
The students are **happy**. The hurricane was **dangerous**.	They are **happy** students. It was a **dangerous** hurricane.

Notes:

- An adjective describes someone or something.
- If there isn't a specific subject, use *it*. Example: *It's hot in the house.*
- Use *very* before the adjective. *Very* makes the adjective stronger. Example: *It was a **very** hot day.*

C Write two sentences about each picture. Use *be* and choose an adjective from the box.

windy	hot	dangerous	yellow	strong
young	sunny	~~thirsty~~	worried	

1. _____He is thirsty._____

_____He is a thirsty man._____

4. _____

_____

2. _____

_____

5. _____

_____

3. _____

_____

6. _____

_____

■ **COMMUNICATE**

D **WRITE** Write a short paragraph about yourself. Compare now to last year. Use adjectives with *be*.

My name is Elian. I am 23 years old. Last year I was in Brazil, but now I am in the United States.

GRAMMAR AND VOCABULARY Work in two small teams. Team 1 thinks of a city, country, or part of the world. Team 2 asks ten questions about location and weather. Use the grammar and vocabulary from this lesson. Team 2 tries to guess Team 1's place. Team 1 gives the answer after ten questions and no correct guess.

PROJECT Prepare a TV weather report.

1. Work in small groups.
2. Choose a country or region you know well. Draw a map of the country and include the major cities.
3. Prepare a TV weather report for the country.
4. Present the report to your class.

 INTERNET Go online and prepare a presentation for your class. Use the keywords "weather around the world" to find the following information:

- the weather today in three cities on three different continents
- the local weather conditions now
- the locations of any hurricanes or tornadoes
- something on a website that you think is interesting

PART 1
Be in the Past: Information
Questions

PART 2
What or *Which* in *Be* Questions

Lesson ②

World History: The 16th Century

■ CONTENT VOCABULARY

Look at the pictures. Do you know the words?

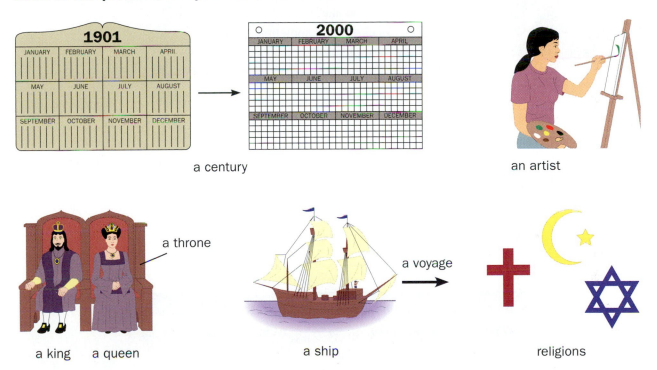

a century

an artist

a throne

a king   a queen

a ship

a voyage

religions

Write the new words in your vocabulary journal.

■ THINK ABOUT IT

Do you know anything that happened in the 16th century? Discuss this question with a partner.

■ GRAMMAR IN CONTENT

CD1,TR3

A **Read and listen.**

Henry VIII

Q: **Who** was Henry VIII?

A: He was the King of England.

Q: **When** was he king?

A: He was king in the 16th century.

Q: **How long** was he king?

A: He was king for 38 years.

Q: **What** was he **like**?

A: He was clever and sometimes cruel.

Q: **Why** is he famous?

A: He is famous because he had six wives.

B **Check (✔) *True* or *False*.**

	True	False
1. Henry VIII was King of England in the 17th century.	☐	☐
2. Henry was king for 38 years.	☐	☐
3. Henry was clever.	☐	☐
4. Henry is famous.	☐	☐

Be in the Present and Past: Information Questions		
Wh- Word / *How* Phrase	*Be*	Noun or Pronoun Phrase
Who	was	the first president?
Where	is	London?
Why	are	you tired?
What	were	their test scores?
When	was	she queen?
How far	is	it to London?
How old	are	you?
How long	was	he king?
How heavy	is	gold?

C (Circle) the correct information word to complete each question about Henry VIII.

1. **Q:** ((When)/ Where) was Henry VIII king?   **A:** In the 16th century.
2. **Q:** (When / Where) was Henry VIII king?   **A:** England.
3. **Q:** (Where / Who) was Catherine of Aragon?   **A:** Henry's first wife.
4. **Q:** (Why / What) was Henry unhappy?   **A:** He didn't have a son.
5. **Q:** (How long / How far) was he king?   **A:** 38 years.

D Read about Magellan. Use the groups of words to write questions with *how*. Write answers to the questions.

Magellan

Ferdinand Magellan was a Portuguese sailor. He was born in 1480. He was the first explorer to sail around the world. When he was 39 years old, he left Spain to go around the world. He took five ships and 270 men. Magellan's ship was the *Trinidad*. It weighed 110 tons. The voyage lasted three years. The ships traveled 69,000 miles. Magellan died in the Philippines. Only 18 men finished the voyage.

1. was / Magellan / at the beginning of the voyage / how old

   Q: _How old was Magellan at the beginning of the voyage?_

   A: _He was 39 years old._

2. men / were / on the ships / how many

   Q: _____

   A: _____

3. ships / how many / were / on the voyage

   Q: _____

   A: _____

4. the *Trinidad* / was / how heavy

   Q: _____

   A: _____

5. how long / the voyage / was

   Q: _____

   A: _____

E Read and listen to the conversation between Cindy and her instructor. Complete Cindy's part of the conversation. Make simple information questions with *be*. Use the instructor's answers to help you.

Instructor:	This is Suleiman the Lawgiver.
Cindy:	*Who was Suleiman* ?
Instructor:	He was a sultan, or king, of the Ottoman Empire.
Cindy:	_____ ?
Instructor:	The Ottoman Empire was in North Africa, Southern Europe, and the Middle East.

Cindy: _____?

Instructor: He was sultan from 1520 to 1566.

Cindy: _____?

Instructor: He was "the Lawgiver" because he made the Ottoman laws.

Cindy: _____?

Instructor: He was a good sultan and a really nice person.

■ **C O M M U N I C A T E**

F **PAIR WORK** Student A looks at the text on this page. Student B looks at the text on page 235. Ask questions to find the answers.

Sofonisba Anguissola was born in _____ (Where?). There were seven children in the family. _____ (How many?) of the children were daughters. Her father was rich. Anguissola was a _____ (What?). She was very famous because she was the first woman artist in Italy. Her sisters were _____ (What?) too. In 1559, she went to Spain. She was a guest of King Philip II. She was very _____ (What?). Later in life she stopped painting because she was blind. She died in 1624. She was 94 years old. Her paintings hang in many galleries. They are in _____ (Where?).

■ GRAMMAR IN CONTENT

A Read and listen.

CD1,TR5

The Aztecs

Bob:	Wow! Look at all these books! **Which book** is for your history class?
Anna:	This one.
Bob:	It's a big book. **What chapter** are you on?
Anna:	The one on civilizations of the 16th century. The Incas and Aztecs.
Bob:	**Which civilization** is more interesting to you?
Anna:	The Aztecs. They had many gods. Look, here's a picture of one.
Bob:	**Which god** is that?
Anna:	Tlaloc, the god of rain.
Bob:	**What country** were the Aztecs from?
Anna:	Mexico.

civilization: a high level of government, laws, culture within a society

B Check (✔) *True* or *False*.

	True	False
1. Anna has a lot of books.	☐	☐
2. Anna knows about many Aztec gods.	☐	☐
3. Tlaloc was the rain god.	☐	☐
4. The Aztecs were from many countries.	☐	☐

What + Noun + *Be*	
What nationality was Henry VIII? **What country** was Henry VIII from?	Use *what* questions to ask someone about something when there is only one answer.

Which + Noun + *Be*	
Which students are in your class? **Which class** was the best?	Use *which* questions to ask someone to identify one thing or person out of many things or people.

C (Circle) *what* or *which* to complete the questions.

1. **A:** Some languages in South America in the 16th century were Maya, Nahuatl, and Otomi.
   B: (Which / What) language was the language of the Aztecs?
   A: Nahuatl.
2. **A:** (Which / What) were the Aztecs' main foods? **B:** Maize, beans, and squash.
3. **A:** (Which / What) city was their capital?   **B:** Tenochtitlan.
4. **A:** (Which / What) art were the Aztecs famous for?   **B:** Poetry.
5. **A:** (Which / What) country ended the Aztecs, Spain or England?   **B:** Spain.

■ **C O M M U N I C A T E**

D **GROUP WORK** Find out the following. Use *which + be* questions.

. . . students are Mexican? . . . students are mothers? . . . students are happy?

Connection | **Putting It Together**

GRAMMAR AND VOCABULARY Work with a classmate. Look at the pictures and information. Write information questions and give complete answers. Discuss who these people were. Use the grammar and vocabulary from the lesson.

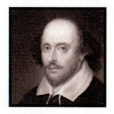

William Shakespeare: playwright, 1564–1616; wrote 38 plays

Michelangelo: artist, 1474–1564; painted the Sistine Chapel, in Rome, Italy

Toyotomi Hideyoshi: ruler, Japan, 1536–1598

 INTERNET PROJECT Go online and make a history test.

1. Work in groups. Research information about the people in this lesson.
2. Create a multiple-choice history quiz using the information you found.
3. Exchange quizzes with another group.
4. When you are finished, correct the other group's quiz.

Earth Science: Geography

■ CONTENT VOCABULARY

Look at the picture. Do you know the words?

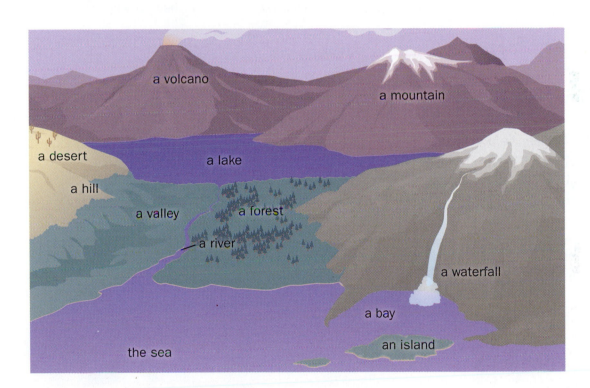

a volcano

a mountain

a desert

a lake

a hill

a valley

a forest

a river

a waterfall

a bay

the sea

an island

Write the new words in your vocabulary journal.

■ THINK ABOUT IT

Which of the following are found in your country? Check (✔) the boxes.

- ☐ volcanoes
- ☐ rivers
- ☐ deserts
- ☐ mountains
- ☐ islands
- ☐ hills
- ☐ lakes
- ☐ forests
- ☐ waterfalls
- ☐ seas
- ☐ bays
- ☐ valleys

■ GRAMMAR IN CONTENT

CD1,TR6

A **Read and listen.**

Surtsey

In 1963 a volcano **under** the sea erupted **near** Iceland. The volcano created a new island called Surtsey. Surtsey is **between** two other volcanic islands. For months the smoke from the volcano was **above** the island. Today, the sea **around** the island is still warm because of the heat from the volcano. Seals often swim **in** the warm waters. Many birds and insects live **on** the island.

Iceland has many islands like Surtsey. After a few hundred years, though, the islands disappear. They are washed away by the sea.

erupted: became violently active

B **Check (✔)** *True* or *False.*

	True	False
1. Surtsey is a volcano.	☐	☐
2. Surtsey is far from Iceland.	☐	☐
3. Animals live on Surtsey.	☐	☐
4. The sea around Surtsey is cold.	☐	☐

Prepositions of Location

in	on	at

A seal is **in** the water.

The seal is **on** the beach.

Many animals live **at** the beach.

next to	above / below	around

The baby is lying **next to** its mother.

Seabirds fly **above** the water to look for fish. The fish are just **below** the surface of the water.

There is water all **around** the island.

far from / near	between	in front of / behind

She wants to keep her baby **far from** the other seals. The baby will be safe if it stays **near** its mother.	The baby seal feels safe lying **between** the two adult seals.	The baby seal is lying **in front of** its mother. The mother seal is lying **behind** her baby.

Notes:

- Use *at* for a general area such as work, school, and home. Example: *Jamie works **at** the airport.*
- Use *in* to talk about a country or city. Example: *I live **in** Boston.*
- Use *on* for things that are next to rivers or bodies of water. Example: *Honolulu is **on** the ocean.*

C (Circle) **the correct preposition to complete these sentences.**

To: mitre@hotdot.net
Subject: We're back!

Hi! We just got back from vacation. It was wonderful! We went to a little village (at / in) Switzerland.
(1)

We stayed (in / at) a small hotel (near / at) the mountains. Our room was (on / in) the second
(2) (3) (4)
floor. The village was very small. We walked (at / around) the village in an hour. The shops
(5)
were not (far from / near) the hotel—only a five-minute walk. The beautiful mountains were
(6)
(behind / on) the village. It was springtime, but there was snow (in / on) those mountains!
(7) (8)
Switzerland is a beautiful country.

Pavel

D Look at the pictures. Fill in each blank below with a preposition from the box.

behind	near	between	on	in	far from

1. **Q:** Where's the house?

   A: It's _____ the river.

2. **Q:** Where are the trees?

   A: They are _____ the house.

3. **Q:** Where's the field?

   A: It's _____ the house and the river.

4. **Q:** Where is the boat?

   A: It's _____ the lake.

5. **Q:** Where are the mountains?

   A: They are _____ the lake.

6. **Q:** Where's Brazil?

   A: It's _____ South America. It's _____ South Africa.

Brazil   South Africa

■ **COMMUNICATE**

E **PAIR WORK** Choose a room in your home. Think of ten things in that room. Describe that room to your partner. Use prepositions of location. Your partner should draw a picture of everything you describe on a piece of paper. Check his or her picture to see if it is correct.

■ **G R A M M A R   I N   C O N T E N T**

CD1,TR7

A **Read and listen.**

Pangaea

A: Three hundred million years ago **there was** just one continent on Earth. It was called Pangaea.

B: Really? **Were there** any seas?

A: Yes, **there were. There was** one big ocean.

B: **Were there** any volcanoes on Pangaea?

A: Yes, **there were** lots of volcanoes.

B: Okay. So, what happened to Pangaea?

A: Over millions of years, Pangaea broke up into seven continents.

B **Check (✔)** *True* or *False*.

	True	False
1. There are eight continents today.	☐	☐
2. There were always seven continents.	☐	☐
3. There weren't volcanoes on Pangaea.	☐	☐
4. There was one big ocean in Pangaea.	☐	☐

There + Be: Statements		
There	**Be**	
There	is / was / isn't / wasn't	a lake.
	are / were	a lot of trees on the mountain.
	aren't / weren't	any trees near the bay.

There + Be: Yes/No Questions			
Be	**There**		**Short Answer**
Is / Was	there	snow? / some snow?	No, there isn't. / No, there wasn't.
Are / Were	there	trees? / any trees?	Yes, there are. / Yes, there were.

Notes:

- *There is* and *There are* mean that something exists (the present).
- *There was* and *There were* mean that something existed (the past).
- In conversational or informal English, many speakers use *There's* for both singular and plural subjects. Examples: **There's** somebody waiting to see you. / **There's** two people waiting to see you.
- With negative *there + be* statements and questions use *any*: **There aren't any fish.**

C Complete the paragraph using *there + be.*

Madeira is a small island near the African coast. Like Surtsey, it started as a volcano. _____There are_____ seven main towns on the island, but _____ only one big city. The city is called Funchal. _____ about 250,000 people on the island. _____ some beaches on Madeira, but _____ no sand, only rocks. _____ many mountains on the island. The biggest is Pico Ruivo. A long time ago, _____ a large forest on the island. But _____ many trees left. _____ tourists all year because the weather is usually warm. Madeira is famous for its nice climate and good wine.

D Write questions for the answers. Use the information in exercise D.

1. **Q:** _____

    A: Yes, there is an island near the African coast.

2. **Q:** _____

    A: Yes, there are many beaches.

3. **Q:** _____

    A: No, there aren't any deserts on Madeira.

4. **Q:** _____

    A: Yes, there are many mountains on Madeira.

5. **Q:** _____

    A: Yes, there was a huge forest on the island.

6. **Q:** _____

    A: Yes, there are many tourists in Maderia.

E Look at the map. Write sentences using *there* + *be* and the words in parentheses.

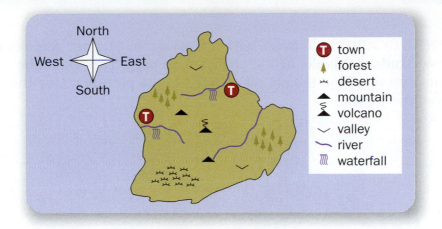

1. (towns) ___ There are two towns on the island. _____

2. (volcanoes) _____

3. (lakes) _____

4. (forest) _____

5. (desert) _____

6. (bay) _____

7. (mountains) _____

8. (valleys) _____

■ **COMMUNICATE**

F **GROUP WORK** Work with two classmates. Ask about a place they know well. Use *there* + *be*.

I'm from Curaçao.

No, there aren't.

Are there mountains on Curaçao?

G Write a paragraph about where you live now. Write another paragraph about where you lived before. Use *there* + *be* in each sentence.

GRAMMAR AND VOCABULARY Work with a classmate. Student A looks at the postcard below. Student B looks at the postcard on page 235. Describe what you both see in the pictures. Find the six differences in the pictures. Use the grammar and vocabulary from the lesson.

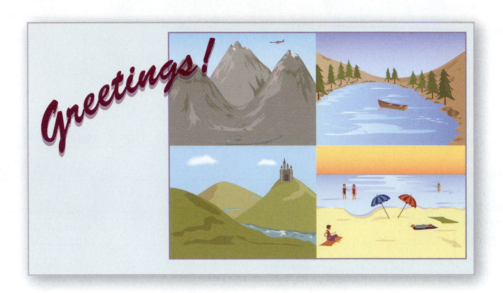

PROJECT Make a poster.

1. Work together with two or three classmates.
2. Make a poster of a map of the area around your school or a map of your school campus.
3. Practice describing everything on your map by using *there is/are* and all the prepositions you know.
4. Present your map to the class and describe everything on it.

 INTERNET Go online. Choose a country you want to know more about. Find out if there are mountains, volcanoes, deserts, lakes, or waterfalls in that country. Report back to your classmates.

PART 1
The Simple Present Tense:
Statements and *Yes/No*
Questions

PART 2
The Simple Present Tense:
Information Questions

Lesson (4)

Business: Globalization

■ CONTENT VOCABULARY

Look at the pictures. Do you know the words?

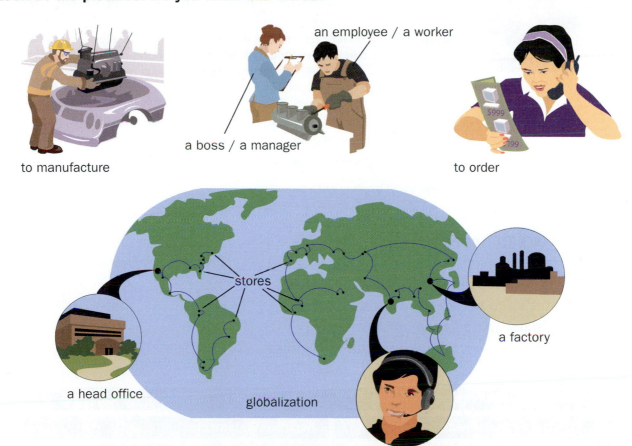

an employee / a worker

a boss / a manager

to manufacture

to order

stores

a head office

globalization

customer service

a factory

Write the new words in your vocabulary journal.

■ THINK ABOUT IT

Name three global companies. What do they do? What do they make? What does globalization mean to you? Discuss these questions with a classmate.

■ GRAMMAR IN CONTENT

A Read and listen to the two college students.

CD1,TR8

The Rally

Sonia: There is an anti-globalization rally today. Do you **want** to go?

Yoshi: I **don't think** so. **Do** you **think** globalization is bad?

Sonia: **Yes, I do.** I **think** globalization is really bad.

Yoshi: But your dad **works** for EnormoCorp. They're the biggest company in the world.

Sonia: My dad **doesn't understand** the problems with globalization. Many people **don't understand** that globalization **hurts** people in both poor and rich countries. Jobs **go** to different countries. People **don't get** good wages. Globalization **helps** companies make more money. It doesn't help people. So, **do** you **want** to come to the rally?

Yoshi: Actually, I can't go. I **work** on Saturday mornings. Also, I'm not sure globalization is bad.

rally: a meeting of people to excite them about an idea

B Check (✔) *True* or *False*.

	True	False
1. Sonia thinks globalization is really bad.	☐	☐
2. Sonia's dad works for EnormoCorp.	☐	☐
3. Yoshi doesn't want to go to the rally.	☐	☐
4. Yoshi doesn't work on Saturday mornings.	☐	☐

Simple Present Tense: Statements					
Affirmative Statements			**Negative Statements**		
Subject	Verb		Subject	*Do Not*	Verb
I You We They	work	in South Korea.	I You We They	do not don't	work in Japan.
He She It	comes	from Mexico.	He She It	does not doesn't	come from Peru.

Simple Present Tense: *Yes/No* Questions and Short Answers

Affirmative Statements				Negative Statements					
Do	**Subject**	**Verb**		**Yes,**	**Subject**	**Do**	**No,**	**Subject**	**Do Not**
Do	I you we they	**work**	in South Korea?	**Yes,**	I you we they	**do.**	**No,**	I you we they	do not. don't.
Does	he she it	**come**	from Mexico?		he she it	**does.**		he she it	does not. doesn't.

Notes:

- Use the simple present to talk about things that:
  1. happen all the time. Example: *Hospital emergency rooms* **treat** *patients.*
  2. are facts. Example: *The sun* **rises** *in the east.*
  3. are habits or routines. Example: *Every day she* **goes** *to work by car.*
- Some verbs use the simple present to talk about states and senses: *like, love, hate, want, believe, know, understand, hear, smell, see, taste.*

C Use the correct form of the verbs in the box to complete these sentences. Change the form of the verb if necessary. You can use a word more than one time.

> not like   work   buy   manufacture   go   not have   live   put   think

Kim ____lives____ in South Korea. He _____ in a factory.
　　　　　(1)　　　　　　　　　　　　　　　(2)
He _____ computer screens. The screens _____ to
　　　(3)　　　　　　　　　　　　　　　　　　(4)
a factory in Ohio in the United States.

Shelly _____ in Ohio. She _____ in a factory, too.
　　　　　(5)　　　　　　　　　　　(6)
She _____ the screens into the computer monitors. She
　　　(7)
_____ her job. She _____ it is boring.
　(8)　　　　　　　　　(9)

The Delgados _____ in Mexico. They _____ a new
　　　　　　　　(10)　　　　　　　　　　　　(11)
computer every three years. Pedro Delgado _____ the PCs
　　　　　　　　　　　　　　　　　　　　　　　(12)
from Shelly's factory in Ohio. The Delgados' town _____ a
　　　　　　　　　　　　　　　　　　　　　　　　　　(13)
computer store. The Delgados order a new computer online.

D Put the words in the right order. Write the questions. Write short answers.

1. work / does / in a factory / Kim?

   Q: _Does Kim work in a factory?_

   A: _Yes, he does. He works in a factory._

2. does / in South Korea / Kim / live?

   Q: _____

   A: _____

3. Shelly / her job / does / like?

   Q: _____

   A: _____

4. in Mexico / live / do / the Delgados?

   Q: _____

   A: _____

5. they / do / a computer every year / buy?

   Q: _____

   A: _____

6. does / a computer store / the town / have?

   Q: _____

   A: _____

E Use the words in the box to write affirmative or negative sentences about yourself. Use the simple present tense.

I	mother	father	my friends	work	study	think	go
want	like	factory	globalization	computer	store	office	

1. _My father works in an office._

2. _____

3. _____

4. _____

5. _____

F **PAIR WORK** Use the words in the box in exercise E to ask your partner questions.

G **GROUP WORK** Write questions with *Do* and *Does.* Ask three of your classmates the questions. Put your classmates' answers in the chart.

Do you have a computer?   Yes, I do. It's a PC.

	Name: _____	Name: _____	Name: _____
1. have / computer? _Do you have a computer?_			
2. use / the Internet? _____			
3. own / a car? _____			
4. work / in a factory? _____			
5. buy / products from your own country? _____			
6. think / globalization is good for everyone? _____			

H **WRITE** Use the information in exercise G to write a short paragraph about one of your classmates.

■ GRAMMAR IN CONTENT

A Read and listen to the following conversation between a newspaper reporter and the CEO, the chief executive officer, of a large, international business.

CD1,TR9

Interview with a CEO

Reporter: **What** does EnormoCorp do?

CEO: We make computers.

Reporter: **How many** employees does EnormoCorp have?

CEO: We have over 12,300 employees.

Reporter: **Where** do your employees work?

CEO: They work in offices and factories around the world.

Reporter: Do you outsource jobs?

CEO: Yes, we do. We outsource jobs to Asia.

Reporter: **Who** works in Asia?

CEO: Many computer technicians work in Asia.

Reporter: **Why** do you outsource work?

CEO: We can pay less to technicians in Asia than in the United States.

Reporter: **What** does globalization mean to you?

CEO: It means that EnormoCorp manufactures the best computers at the best price.

CEO: Chief Executive Officer, the most important person in a company

outsource: to use people outside a company to do work or service

price: cost, an amount of money charged for goods or services

B Check (✔) *True* or *False*.

	True	False
1. EnormoCorp makes all kinds of electronics.	☐	☐
2. EnormoCorp outsources jobs to Europe.	☐	☐
3. EnormoCorp has offices all over the world.	☐	☐
4. Computer technicians in this country and Asia get the same wage.	☐	☐

Simple Present: Information Questions				
Wh- Words / How Phrases	Object	Do	Subject	Verb
		do	I you we they	have?
What How many	offices	—————		
		does	he she it	

Simple Present: Information Questions			
Wh- Words	Do	Subject	Verb
What Which Who(m)	do	I you we they	like?
Where When Why	does	he she it	work?

Subject	Verb	Answer
Who	**makes** cars?	Many factories do.
What	**happens** to the screens?	They go to an American factory.

Notes:

- *Wh-* words and *how* phrases are used for information questions.
- *Whom* can be used as the object in formal speaking and writing.
- Don't use the auxiliary *do* or *does* with *who* or *what* when they are the <u>subject</u> of the question.
  Example: *Who likes globalization?* (*Who* is the subject, so don't use the auxiliary.)

C (Circle) **the correct form of *do* in the following questions.**

1. Where (do / (does)) Panjit work?
2. Who (do / does) Joe and Maggie think is a good worker?
3. When (do / does) Manuel have his meeting?
4. How much (do / does) a computer cost?
5. What (do / does) you think about globalization?

D Read each sentence below. Each sentence has one error. Correct each error.

1. What ~~does make~~ *makes* globalization good and bad?

2. How much money our company save?

3. What computer you like, Mr. Park?

4. Where they get their auto parts?

5. Who do speak against globalization?

E Look at the <u>underlined</u> part of each answer. Write information questions.

1. Q: _Why do you go to work, Berta?_

   A: I go to work <u>because I love my job.</u>

2. Q: _____

   A: I work <u>in an office.</u>

3. Q: _____

   A: The office opens <u>at 8:00.</u>

4. Q: _____

   A: My office is <u>9 feet by 12 feet.</u>

5. Q: _____

   A: I have lunch <u>at 12:30.</u>

6. Q: _____

   A: I work <u>eight hours every day.</u>

7. Q: _____

   A: <u>No one.</u> I don't know anyone at work yet.

F Complete the following conversation. Use the word(s) in parentheses. Add *do* or *does* if necessary. Some sentences may need a negative.

Helen: What company _____ (your father/work) for, Sanjay?
(1)

Sanjay: For Earthnet Technologies.

Helen: How many people _____ (work) there?
(2)

Sanjay: I think 700, Helen. It's not a very big company.

Helen: How many companies _____ (Earthnet/help) with outsourcing?
(3)

Sanjay: I'm sorry. What's the question?

Helen: How many companies _____ (outsource) work to Earthnet?
(4)

Sanjay: I _____ (know) how many, Helen. I _____ (work) there.
(5)   (6)

■ C O M M U N I C A T E

G **PAIR WORK** Student B, turn to page 236. Student A, ask Student B questions to complete the information about Basia. Student B, ask Student A questions to complete the information about Panjit.

Panjit
(who) CompuLab, Inc.
(what) computer technician
(where) New Delhi, India
(how much) $25 per hour
(why) likes computers

Basia
(who) FabriCare, Inc.
(what) seamstress
(where) Moscow, Russia
(how much) $5 per hour
(why) likes her coworkers

GRAMMAR AND VOCABULARY Write two *yes/no* questions and three information questions about the following topics. Use the grammar and vocabulary from the lesson. Then, ask a classmate the questions. Write down his or her answers. Then, report back to your class.

Do you like globalization?

Yes, I do. I think it's good for people.

school   work   business   ~~globalization~~   your usual day

Question	Answer
1. Do you like globalization?	
2.	
3.	
4.	
5.	

PROJECT Write a letter to the editor.

- Work with two or three classmates.
- Write a short letter to the editor of a newspaper.
- Write the reasons you are for or against globalization.
- Add new facts that you found on the Internet.
- Show your finished letter to the class.

 INTERNET Go online. Use the keywords "globalization facts" to find five interesting facts about globalization. Write those facts in your notebook.

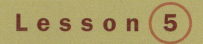

Lesson ⑤

Anthropology: Cultural Diversity

■ CONTENT VOCABULARY

Look at the pictures. Do you know the words?

to smile

to touch

to shake hands

to kiss

to retire

to get married

Write the new words in your vocabulary journal.

■ THINK ABOUT IT

Do you know people from different cultures? Do they have different customs? Discuss the questions in a small group.

■ GRAMMAR IN CONTENT

CD1,TR10

A Read and listen to the following conversation between a restaurant customer and a server.

Cultural Misunderstandings

Nora: [snapping her fingers] Psst! Psst!

Server: Are you talking to me? You know, people **usually** say, "Excuse me." And they **never** snap their fingers. It's rude to do that.

Nora: Oh, sorry. Excuse me. You must get me a breakfast menu.

Server: Must? Listen, dear, servers **seldom** respond to orders like that. **Always** say, "May I have a menu?" Okay?

Nora: Okay. Sorry. I'm new to the United States.

Server: Yes, I know. Would you like something to drink? Juice? Coffee?

Nora: I **occasionally** drink coffee, but not **often**.

Server: I **sometimes** drink tea. Would you like some tea this morning?

Nora: Yes, please. And thank you for the culture lesson.

Server: You're welcome.

misunderstanding: a mistaken idea   **to respond:** react, answer   **order:** a command

B Check (✔) *True* or *False*.

	True	False
1. People in restaurants usually say "Excuse me" to servers for attention.	☐	☐
2. Servers in restaurants always respond to strong orders.	☐	☐
3. Nora sometimes drinks coffee.	☐	☐
4. The server always drinks coffee.	☐	☐

Adverbs of Frequency		Notes:
Adverbs	**Examples**	• Put adverbs of frequency after the verb *be*.
100% **Always**	I **am always** curious about cultures.	• Put adverbs of frequency before all other verbs.
Almost always		
Usually	You **usually ask** me questions.	
Often / Frequently	She **is frequently** late for work.	
Sometimes / Occasionally	His opinions **were occasionally** strong.	
Rarely / Seldom		
Almost never	We **are rarely** bored by other cultures.	
0% **Never**	They **never understand** us.	

C Complete the paragraph. Rewrite each sentence. Put the adverb of frequency (in parentheses) in the correct place.

A Guide to American Manners

Americans ___always like___ (like, always) to be punctual. They _____ (be, usually) on
          (1)   (2)
time for work, meetings, and appointments.

Americans _____ (be, almost always) polite. In a conversation, they
                    (3)

_____ (stand, rarely) very near to each other. Also, people _____ (look,
       (4)   (5)
usually) each other in the eye when they talk or listen. They _____ (turn, never) their eyes
                                                                      (6)
away from the speaker.

Be careful! Americans _____ (ask, seldom) other people about their finances. It is rude
                              (7)
to ask how much money someone earns. They _____ (ask, sometimes) a person's age,
                                                      (8)
but only for special reasons.

Americans _____ (smile, always) in photographs. They _____ (be, always)
                  (9)   (10)
ready to smile when they say, "Hello."

D Use the words in parentheses to answer the questions. Write short answers and statements.

1. Do friends in India usually kiss each other on the cheek when they meet?

   (No, / rarely) _____ No, they don't. They rarely kiss each other
   ___ on the cheek when they meet. _____

2. Do friends in Italy touch each other when they talk?

   (Yes, / often) _____

   _____

3. Do people in Japan take off their shoes before they enter somebody's house?

   (Yes, / always) _____

   _____

4. Does an American man give a ring to the woman who agrees to marry him?

(Yes, / usually) _____

_____

5. In some Middle Eastern and Asian countries, does a woman usually show her face to men not in her family?

(No, / never) _____

_____

■ COMMUNICATE

E **WRITE** Write a paragraph about manners in your culture or the country you live in. What is polite? What is rude? Use adverbs of frequency.

| PART TWO | Prepositions of Time |

■ GRAMMAR IN CONTENT

A Read the passage.

Some Interesting Cross-Cultural Facts

- Many cultures say you cannot marry **before** you're 16 years old. But in other cultures, you can marry **at** the age of 12.

- In some cultures, children have their own apartments **by** the age of 21. In other cultures, children don't leave their parents' home **before** they get married.

- People eat a salad **before** a meal in some countries. In other countries, people eat a salad **after** a meal.

- Many cultures have their big meal **in** the afternoon. But other cultures have their big meal **in** the evening.

- People are finished with dinner **by** 7:00 PM in some countries. In other countries, people are finished with dinner **at** midnight.

- People in many countries work **from** Monday **to** Friday. In other countries, people work six or even seven days a week.

B Check (✔) True or False.

	True	False
1. Not all cultures say you must be 16 years old to get married.	☐	☐
2. People around the world eat dinner at 7:00 PM.	☐	☐
3. Nobody works from Monday to Saturday.	☐	☐
4. Some people eat a salad before a meal. Others eat it after a meal.	☐	☐

Prepositions of Time

at night at 6:00 at age six	**Notes:** Use *at* with a specific time or age. Example: *In the West, many people start work **at** 6:00 AM.*
on Saturday **on** New Year's Day	Use *on* with days and holidays. Example: *They got married **on** January 18.*
in the morning **in** 30 minutes	Use *in* for a long or short period of time. Example: *For many people, breakfast is a quick meal. They are finished **in** 30 minutes.*
by 6:00 **by** age 30	Use *by* before a specific time or at that specific time, but not after that time. Example: *It is very unusual in many cultures if a person is not married **by** the age of 30.*
from 12:00 to 1:00	Use *from . . . to . . .* to show the limits (start and end) of a time period. Examples: *In some countries, many people have lunch **from** 12:00 **to** 1:00. / A school year for many children is **from** September **to** June.*
before / **after**	*In most cultures, people get married **before** they have children. In most cultures, people have children **after** they get married.*

C Use prepositions of time to complete the sentences.

1. Russians celebrate May Day __*on*__ May 1.

2. Australians celebrate Christmas _____ the summer.

3. Americans can vote _____ the age of 18.

4. In the Gregorian calendar, a new year starts _____ midnight _____ January 1.

5. _____ lunch, many Spaniards take a siesta and then go back to work.

6. In Poland, children go to school _____ the age of 7 _____ the age of 18.

7. Muslims have their Sabbath _____ Friday.

8. Most Greeks go on vacation _____ August.

D **PAIR WORK** Discuss a country you know well. Talk about the things below. Use prepositions of time.

1. when people retire
2. when they start school
3. how long they attend college
4. when they get married
5. when they celebrate holidays

Connection | Putting It Together

GRAMMAR AND VOCABULARY Work in groups. Ask and answer questions using the words below. Use the grammar and vocabulary from this lesson. Ask each classmate, "What's something you _____ do _____?"

> What's something you <u>rarely</u> do <u>on Sundays</u>?

> I <u>rarely</u> cook <u>on Sundays</u>. I usually go out for dinner.

always / in the evening
usually / on Sundays
sometimes / before bedtime
rarely / from 3:00 AM to 4:00 AM
never / after class

PROJECT Interview a classmate.

1. Choose a classmate.
2. Interview your classmate. Find out about his/her daily life, what he/she does, where he/she lives.
3. Write a paragraph saying how your daily life is different from your classmate's.

 INTERNET Choose a culture you want to know more about. Go online. Find information about that culture. What do people usually do in their daily lives? What are considered some good and bad manners in that culture? Tell the class what you find.

A Complete the sentences. In some blanks, use the verbs in parentheses. In other blanks, put something that completes the ideas.

From: Ailton@brazlink.net
To: Cclovis@worldview.co.uk
Cc:
Subject: Some News for You

Hi, Clive!

How _____ life? _____ London this summer? I _____ sure _____ hot,
　　　(1)　　　　　　　(2)　　　　　　　　　　　　　　(3)　　　　　　(4)

right? _____ you know where I am? No, not _____ Rio de Janeiro! I'm very
　　　　(5)　　　　　　　　　　　　　　　　　　　(6)

_____ _____ Rio, 1000s of miles away. _____ a famous statue here, the Statue
　(7)　　　　(8)　　　　　　　　　　　　　　　　(9)

of Liberty. _____ that help you? The place _____ New York City, Clive!
　　　　　　(10)　　　　　　　　　　　　　(11)

I arrived _____ June _____ English classes! I (take)_____ classes _____
　　　　　(12)　　　　　　(13)　　　　　　　　　　　　(14)　　　　　　　　(15)

Mondays, Wednesdays, and Thursdays. I (have) _____ two classes _____ those days.
　　　　　　　　　　　　　　　　　　　　(16)　　　　　　　　(17)

The morning class (start) _____ _____ 9:00 A.M. and (end)_____ _____
　　　　　　　　　　　　(18)　　　　(19)　　　　　　　　　　　(20)　　　　(21)

noon. The afternoon class (be)_____ _____ 1:00 P.M. _____ 3:00 P.M.
　　　　　　　　　　　　　　(22)　　　　(23)　　　　　　　(24)

We (go) _____ to lunch _____ the morning class. And the teacher _____ very
　　　(25)　　　　　　　　(26)　　　　　　　　　　　　　　　　　　　(27)

good. She _____ a New Yorker. _____ 19 students _____ my class at the
　　　　　(28)　　　　　　　　　　(29)　　　　　　　(30)

beginning of the program, but now _____ only 16 students. The students (come) _____
　　　　　　　　　　　　　　　　(31)　　　　　　　　　　　　　　　　　　　(32)

_____ many countries. _____ of us meet _____ the cafeteria for breakfast
　(33)　　　　　　　　　　(34)　　　　　　　(35)

_____ class. _____ 3 o'clock, _____ classes, we (walk) _____ all
　(36)　　　　　　(37)　　　　　　　(38)　　　　　　　　　　　(39)

_____ New York together and see interesting things.
　(40)

I hope to hear from you soon.

Ailton

B Complete the sentences. Some blanks have verbs in parentheses. If you see a blank with no verb, think of something to put there.

From: Cclovis@worldview.co.uk
To: Ailton@brazlink.net
Cc:
Subject: I Love New York!

Wow, what a big surprise, Ailton! New York _____ a great place to be. I _____ there
                                                    (1)   (2)

last summer. It _____ a great place to learn English, too! _____ lots of language
                        (3)   (4)

schools _____ the city. _____ school (be) _____ you _____?
              (5)   (6)   (7)   (8)

_____ (be) _____ the name of the school? I (need) _____ _____ classes,
     (9)   (10)   (11)   (12)

too! British English and American English (be) _____ exactly the same, you know.
                                                      (13)

I (understand) _____ 100% of American English. I (want) _____ to ask you a lot of
                    (14)   (15)

questions, my friend, but I (have) _____ much time. _____ your teacher speak only in
                                        (16)   (17)

English to the students? _____ (give) _____ you lots of trouble, grammar or
                               (18)   (19)

vocabulary? _____ (be) _____ your English program? _____ it last only two
                  (20)   (21)   (22)

months? And _____ (be) _____ the school? _____ it _____ Central Park
                  (23)   (24)   (25)   (26)

or the Empire State Building?

  Write soon, my friend!

  Clive

LEARNER LOG Check (✔) *Yes* or *I Need More Practice.*

Lesson	I Can Use . . .	Yes	I Need More Practice
1	The Present and Past of *Be*; *Be* with Nouns or Adjectives		
2	Information Questions in the Present and Past with *Be*; *What* and *Which* in *Be* Questions		
3	Prepositions of Location; *There is/are* and *There was/were*		
4	The Simple Present Tense in Statements, *Yes/No* Questions, and Information Questions		
5	Adverbs of Frequency; Prepositions of Time		

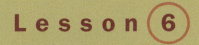

PART 1
Possessive Nouns

PART 2
Possessive Adjectives;
Possessive Pronouns; Questions
with *Whose*

L e s s o n (6)

Sociology: Blended Families

■ CONTENT VOCABULARY

Look at the pictures. Do you know the words?

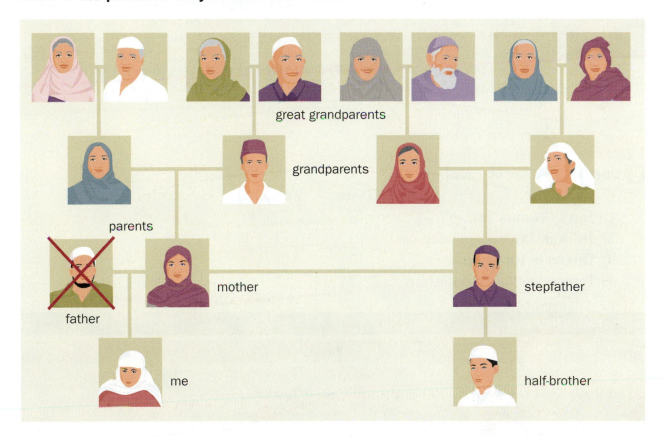

great grandparents

grandparents

parents

father

mother

stepfather

me

half-brother

Write the new words in your vocabulary journal.

■ THINK ABOUT IT

Are large families common in your country? Are families getting smaller in your country? Discuss.

■ **GRAMMAR IN CONTENT**

A Read and listen to the description of this family tree.

CD1,TR11

> ### A Blended Family
>
> Jan is 15 years old. Jan's family is a little complicated. His father and his mother Rita divorced two years ago. Last year Rita remarried. Rita's new husband's name is Tomas. Tomas has a daughter called Julia. Julia is Jan's stepsister. Recently, Tomas and Rita had a new baby. The baby is Jan and Julia's half-brother.
>
> We call this kind of family a *blended family*. Most blended families are successful. But some children in blended families find it difficult. Jan's father let him stay out until 10 PM, but Tomas says he should be home by 9 PM. A stepfather's role is difficult too. For example, Tomas isn't sure how strict he can be with Jan.
>
> Sociologists say that by 2010 there will be more blended families than any other type of family in the United States.

strict: expecting rules to be followed

B Check (✔) *True* or *False*.

	True	False
1. Jan is Tomas' father.	☐	☐
2. Julia is Jan's stepsister.	☐	☐
3. Tomas is Rita's wife.	☐	☐
4. Tomas is Jan's stepfather.	☐	☐

Possessive Nouns

Nouns	Rule	Examples
Singular nouns (living things)	add 's	Sam is **Julia's** husband.
Singular nouns (that end in s)	add ' or 's	Mr. **Jones'** (or **Jones's**) children are nice.
Plural nouns (regular)	add '	Michael's **parents'** names are Sam and Julia.
Plural nouns (irregular)	add 's	The **men's** names are Sam, Michael, and Cliff.
Any noun when possession is understood	add 's	I'm going to my **cousin's** tonight. = I'm going to my **cousin's** house tonight.

Notes:

- When two or more people are mentioned as the possessors, only the last name needs to have the 's on it. Example: ***Sam and Julia's*** *son is Michael.*

- In hyphenated words the 's comes at the end. Example: *That hat is my son-in-law's.*

C Use the words in parentheses to complete each sentence with a possessive phrase.

(Julia) _____Julia's_____ family is blended. (Julia) _____

husband is Des. (Des) _____ son is Cliff. (Julia) _____

daughter is Dora. Dora is (Michael) _____ half-sister.

(Des and Julia) _____ children live together. Des and Julia have twin

daughters. The (twin) _____ names are Tilly and Milly. A blended

(family) _____ life can be complicated.

■ COMMUNICATE

D **PAIR WORK** Work with a classmate. Ask your classmate questions to find out about his/her family. Use possessive nouns in your questions when possible.

 What are your parents' names?

 Their names are Najib and Aisha.

PART TWO	Possessive Adjectives; Possessive Pronouns; Questions with *Whose*

■ GRAMMAR IN CONTENT

CD1,TR12

A Read and listen.

My Blended Family

Hans: Do you want to see some photos?

Kobe: Sure. Who's that?

Hans: That's **my** half-sister Joanne.

Kobe: **Whose** car is that? Is it your sister's car?

Hans: No, it's not **hers**. It's **my** stepfather's.

Kobe: He really needs to change **its** color. Purple looks awful! Who are the two boys?

Hans: They are **my** half-brothers. **Their** names are Jorge and Ricardo. They're twins!

Kobe: Is this **their** house?

Hans: No, it isn't **theirs**. It's **mine**. I share it with **my** grandson.

Kobe: **Your** family is so interesting!

	True	False
1. Juan is Joanne's brother.	☐	☐
2. The car doesn't belong to Joanne.	☐	☐
3. Jorge and Ricardo are Joanne's brothers.	☐	☐
4. Hans lives alone.	☐	☐

Possessive Adjectives and Pronouns

Subject Pronouns	Possessive Adjectives	Possessive Pronouns	Examples
I	my	mine	**My** name is Shirley. **Her** name is Shirley. **Mine** is Michael.
you	your	yours	**Your** sister is intelligent. Thanks. **Yours** is, too.
he	his	his	**His** father is very nice. I know. **His** is nicer than mine.
she	her	hers	**Her** sister has one son. I know your little boy, but I don't know **hers**.
it	its		Did you see that cat? **Its** body is all white.
we	our	ours	**Our** family isn't very large. Maybe yours isn't, but **ours** certainly is!
they	their	theirs	**Their** father works for an auto company. My father doesn't make as much money as **theirs**.

Notes:

• Possessive adjectives show that something belongs to someone. Possessive pronouns also show that something belongs to someone.

• Possessive pronouns replace possessive adjectives and the nouns that follow them.
Example: *Steven's parents are on vacation.* **Ours** *aren't.* (or **Our parents** *aren't on vacation.*)

Questions with *Whose*

Whose	Answer with Possessive
Whose car is this?	Mine. It's mine. It's my car.
Whose parents are divorced?	His. Jan's. Jan's are. Jan's parents are divorced.

Notes:

• Questions with *Whose* are different from *Who is. Whose* asks who owns something.

• Always keep *whose* + noun together. Example: **Whose** *book is this?* NOT: **Whose** *is this book?*

C **Fill in the blanks to complete these short dialogues. Use possessive adjectives, possessive pronouns, and *whose*.**

1. **A:** Is this the Fontaines'?

   B: Yes, it's ___their___ house.

   A: Aha! I was sure it was ___theirs___.

2. **A:** Does the house in this photo belong to your sister?

   B: Yes, it's _____ house.

3. **A:** _____ photos are these?

   B: They are _____. I'm giving them to you.

4. **A:** Is this your dog?

   B: No, it isn't. I thought it was _____! _____ dog is it?

   A: I don't know. It isn't _____.

5. **A:** I don't recognize that large SUV in the driveway. _____ car is it?

   B: It belongs to Mr. and Mrs. Gomez.

   A: Are you sure it's _____ car?

   B: Yes, it's _____.

D **Circle the correct possessive adjective or pronoun.**

1. Gloria is (**my** / mine) sister. The size of (our / ours) families is different. There are only four people in (my / mine), but there are seven in (her / hers).

2. (Our / Ours) house is large, but Gloria's house is much larger. (Her / Hers) has two more bedrooms than (our / ours).

3. Gloria and her husband Frank are very proud of (their / theirs) children. (My / Mine) husband and (my / I) are proud of (our / ours), too.

4. What about (your / yours) family? Is (your / yours) large or small? And what about the size of (your / yours) house? Is it like (my / mine), or is it really large like Gloria's?

E **WRITE** Write a paragraph about things that your family owns. Use possessive adjectives and pronouns.

> I have a very large family. My parents' house is in Princeton, New Jersey. My grandparents live in Lima, Peru. Their home is beautiful.

Connection | Putting It Together

GRAMMAR AND VOCABULARY Compare some people on your father's side of the family with some people on your mother's side. Use the vocabulary and grammar in this lesson for your comparisons. Write them in your notebook.

> My father's mother was a housewife. Her job was not easy. She raised six children. My mother's mother was a teacher. She raised four children, and she worked with other people's children. I think hers was a more difficult job.

PROJECT Create a family tree.

1. First work by yourself.
2. Create your own family tree on a page in your notebook. Use the charts in Part One to guide you. Try to show at least four generations of your family.
3. Then work with a classmate. Take turns showing your family trees to each other. Explain who all those people are and their connections to you. Ask each other questions about the people in the family trees.

 INTERNET Go online. Do research on genealogical organizations. These groups are interested in genealogies, the names and histories of families. Find out some interesting facts about one of these organizations. Write the information in your notebook. Tell your class about that organization.

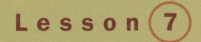

Business:
Buying and Selling

■ **CONTENT VOCABULARY**

Look at the pictures. Do you know the words?

to import/ship

goods

a price

to buy

to sell

to rise   to fall

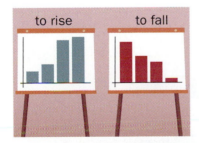

to make a loss   to make a profit

Write the new words in your vocabulary journal.

■ **THINK ABOUT IT**

How do goods from other countries come to stores where you live? How do stores decide on the prices for the goods they sell? Discuss this with the class.

■ **GRAMMAR IN CONTENT**

CD1,TR13

A Read the following passage about importing.

> ### An Imports Business
>
> Jules and Irene have a company called Antiques Inc. **It** imports antiques from other countries. Jules is very good at choosing antiques. Irene knows antiques, too. **They** make a good team. Irene is a great salesperson. **She** is very good at selling. Jules travels all over the world. When **he** sees beautiful antiques, **he** buys **them** at the best price he can get **them.** Then he ships them to New York.
>
> Irene puts the new antiques in their store and raises the prices. **She** sells **them** to buyers. Antiques Inc. makes a profit. The buyers like doing business with **her. They** raise the price again to make a profit.

antiques: objects that are very valuable because they are old

B Check (✔) *True* or *False.*

	True	False
1. Antiques Inc. imports computers.	☐	☐
2. Jules and Irene work well together.	☐	☐
3. Buyers get antiques at factory prices.	☐	☐
4. In stores, we pay a lot more for something than importers pay.	☐	☐

Personal Pronouns

Subject Form	I	you	he	she	it	we	they
Object Form	me	you	him	her	it	us	them

Notes:

- Use personal pronouns in place of people's names or nouns. Example: *I saw **Carla** an hour ago.* → *I saw **her** an hour ago.*
- The subject does the action. Example: ***She** is helping him.*
- The object receives the action. Example: *She is helping **him.***
- After a preposition, use the object form: Example: *She is selling a vase <u>to</u> **him.***
- When identifying somebody by saying *It's . . .* or *That's . . .,* use the object form of the personal pronoun. Example: *"Who is it?" "It's **me.** Unlock the door, please."*

C (Circle) the correct form for each pronoun.

Irene is waiting for a call. Jules calls (she /(her)) at 3:00 PM.

(He / Him) is calling from a factory in Italy. There is a problem with

the factory. (They / them) shipped some vases a month ago. Irene

doesn't think (they / them) sent (they / them). She says, "I don't think

the factory shipped the goods to (we / us)." Jules wants to see the invoices that show

the factory shipped the goods. If Jules sees (they / them), he will know that the factory

is telling the truth. "I'm sure that the factory isn't lying to (we / us)," Jules says.

D Complete the conversation between Jules and Aldo, a factory owner in Italy. Use personal pronouns.

Aldo: Good to see you again, Jules! How are you? And Irene?

Jules: _____I_____ am fine, thanks, Aldo. And _____ is, too. How's
              (1)   **(2)**

              your family?

Aldo: _____'re all very well, thank you. So, Jules, how can _____
              (3)   **(4)**

              help _____ today?
                      (5)

Jules: Can _____ show _____ your new goods?
                    (6)   **(7)**

Aldo: With pleasure! _____'re beautiful vases, Jules. _____ will
                              (8)   **(9)**

              like _____ very much.
                      (10)

Jules: Oh! _____ really are beautiful! _____'re right, Aldo. Irene will
                    (11)   **(12)**

              love _____! _____ will want to have _____ in our store.
                      (13)   **(14)**   **(15)**

Aldo: Fantastic!

Jules: You know what, Aldo? _____ would like ten crates of these vases.
                                      (16)

              Please ship _____ to _____ as soon as possible for our New
                            (17)   **(18)**

              York store.

Aldo: Okay, Jules. Will do.

■ **COMMUNICATE**

E **PAIR WORK** Ask a partner about a special item they own. Ask about where the object is from, how old it is, where the object is now, and why it's special.

■ GRAMMAR IN CONTENT

CD1,TR14

A Listen to and read the following conversation between Irene and Neil, a buyer for a large chain of gift shops. They're in Irene's showroom.

Making a Sale

Irene:	So, Neil, do you see anything you like?
Neil:	I really like the vases. I think our stores will sell many of **them**.
Irene:	Great. This **one** is glass. We also have a green **one** and a gold-colored **one**.
Neil:	Fine. I'll buy two glass vases. If **they** sell, we'll buy some other **ones**, too.
Irene:	I'm sure **they**'ll sell fast, Neil.
Neil:	By the way, can I take this vase with me today?
Irene:	I'm sorry, Neil, but **it**'s the only **one** I have in the showroom.
Neil:	That's okay.

One, Ones, It, Them/They

one	Does she have **an invoice?**	Yes, she has **one**. (*one* = an invoice)	*One* takes the place of *a/an* + singular noun. Use it to avoid repetition.
	Do you have a **blue vase?**	No, but I have **a green one**. (*one* = a vase)	*One* takes the place of *a/an* + adjective + noun.
ones	Do they make **blue dishes?**	No, they only make **black ones.** (*ones* = dishes)	*Ones* takes the place of plural noun when we use adjective + plural noun.
it	Where did you put **the check?**	I left **it** on your desk. (*it* = the check)	*It* takes the place of *the* + singular noun.
	Do you have **her phone number?**	Yes, I have **it**. (*it* = her phone number)	*It* takes the place of possessive adjective + singular noun.
them / they	Where did you put **the invoices?**	I left **them** on your desk. (*them* = the invoices) **They** are on your desk. (*they* = the invoices)	*Them/they* takes the place of *the* + plural noun.
	Did you write down **their phone numbers?**	Yes, I have **them** in my wallet. (*them* = their phone numbers) Yes, **they** are in my wallet. (*they* = their phone numbers)	*Them/they* takes the place of possessive adjective + plural noun.

B Check (✔) *True* or *False*.

	True	False
1. Irene shows three different vases.	☐	☐
2. Neil works for a department store.	☐	☐
3. Neil wants one vase.	☐	☐
4. Irene is selling Neil eight pieces today.	☐	☐

C Fill in the blanks with *one*, *ones*, *it*, or *they*.

1. the Greek statue _the Greek one_   5. the cheap toys   _____

2. an old painting _____   6. the companies   _____

3. four new items _____   7. a good copy   _____

4. the showroom _____   8. the factory   _____

D Rewrite each sentence using *one*, *ones*, *it*, or *they (them)*. Keep adjectives.

1. We will order more of <u>the platters</u> if we sell the old <u>platters</u>.

   We will order more of them if we sell the old ones.

2. They had a rug in the showroom, but they sold <u>the rug</u> last week.

   _____

3. We don't have silver lamps, but we have <u>bronze</u> lamps and <u>copper</u> lamps.

   _____

4. <u>The shipping department</u> made a mistake with <u>our invoices</u>.

   _____

5. All of <u>the new products</u> will be in <u>our catalog</u> next month.

   _____

■ **COMMUNICATE**

E **PAIR WORK** Interview a classmate. Ask and answer questions about things you own. Use *one*, *ones*, *it*, and *they* in your questions and answers.

Do you have any televisions?

We have a large one in the living room and a small one in our bedroom.

GRAMMAR AND VOCABULARY In your notebook, write a short paragraph about a store you know well. Use the grammar and vocabulary from the lesson.

PROJECT Be a buyer.

1. Work with two classmates. You are buyers for a large department store chain. Your job is to choose imported vases and artificial flowers that will look pretty in the vases. Your stores will sell the arrangements.
2. Look at the vases of flowers below. Choose the vases that you think will sell well.
3. Decide which flowers should go into the vases. Some vases may have only one kind of flower. Some may have combinations of flowers.
4. Use *one, ones, it,* and *they (them)* in your discussion.
5. Prepare a presentation for the whole class. They are your customers. Do your best to sell the vases and flower arrangements to your customers.

 INTERNET Go online. Search for one of the following: antique jewelry, antique coins, antique furniture. Find an item you like. Write down the information about the item. Tell the class about your "special find."

PART 1
The Present Progressive Tense:
Statements, *Yes/No* Questions,
Short Answers

PART 2
The Present Progressive Tense:
Information Questions

L e s s o n ⑧

Physical Science:
Astronomy

■ CONTENT VOCABULARY

Look at the pictures. Do you know the words?

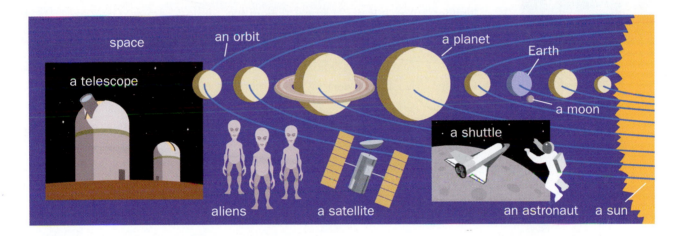

space an orbit a planet Earth
a telescope a moon
aliens a satellite a shuttle an astronaut a sun

Write the new words in your vocabulary journal.

■ THINK ABOUT IT

Astronomers find new things all the time. What are they looking for? Think of two or three things. Discuss your ideas with a classmate.

■ GRAMMAR IN CONTENT

CD1,TR15

A **Read and listen.**

planetoid: an object that is like a planet

Inuit: the native people who live near the Arctic

A New Discovery

Karen:	**Are** you still **working?**
Jennifer:	Yes, I **am.** At the moment I**'m looking** at a new planetoid.
Karen:	Really? What's its name?
Jennifer:	Astronomers **are calling** it Sedna.
Karen:	That's an interesting name. **Are** they **naming** it for a scientist?
Jennifer:	**No, they aren't.** Sedna's the Inuit goddess of the sea. The Inuit say that Sedna lives at the bottom of the Arctic Ocean.
Karen:	**Is** Sedna **orbiting** our sun?
Jennifer:	**Yes,** it **is.** It's a long way from the sun in a very cold part of space. It**'s moving** very slowly. It takes 11,500 years to orbit the sun.
Karen:	Can I take a look? **Is** that telescope **working?**
Jennifer:	No, it **isn't working** at the moment, but this one**'s working.**
Karen:	Oh, no! The **sky's getting** cloudy. I can't see it.
Jennifer:	Never mind. You can look at it tomorrow night. Sedna will be in the sky for a long time.

B **Check (✔) *True* or *False*.**

	True	False
1. Jennifer is looking at a moon.	☐	☐
2. Astronomers are using the name of an Inuit leader for the planet.	☐	☐
3. Sedna is orbiting the sun.	☐	☐
4. Both telescopes are working.	☐	☐

Present Progressive: Affirmative and Negative Statements					
Affirmative Statements			**Negative Statements**		
Subject	**Be**	**Verb + -ing**	**Subject**	**Be + Not**	**Verb + -ing**
I	am	**reading** about Sedna.	I	am not	**reading** about Mars.
He She It	is	**orbiting** Earth.	He She It	is not	**orbiting** the moon.
You We They	are	**studying** astronomy.	You We They	are not	**studying** biology.

Yes/No Questions			Short Answers
Be	**Subject**	**Verb + -ing**	
Are	you	**reading** about Sedna?	Yes, I **am**. No, I **am not**./No, I'm not.
Am	I	**studying** astronomy?	Yes, you **are**. No, you **are not**. No, you're **not**. / No, you **aren't**.
Is	he she it	**going** away?	Yes, he/she/it **is**. No, he/she/it **is not**. No, he's/she's/it's **not**. No, he/she/it **isn't**.
Are	we	**learning** about Sedna?	Yes, we **are**. No, we **are not**. No, we're **not**. / No, we **aren't**.
Are	they	**orbiting** Earth?	Yes, they **are**. No, they **are not**. No, they're **not**. /No, they **aren't**.

Note:

Use the present progressive to talk about something that is happening (or is not happening) right now.

C Complete the conversation. Use the words in parentheses. Use the contracted forms of the present progressive. Use affirmative and negative forms.

Cory: Hey, Sue! _____*Are you going*_____ (you / go) to the computer room?

Sue: Yes, _____ (I / be). I _____

(write) an essay about Sedna.

Cory: Sedna? What's Sedna?

Sue: Some astronomers say it's the ninth planet in the solar system.

Cory: A ninth planet? _____ (you / kid)?

Sue: No, _____ (I / not be). They

_____ (call) it Sedna in honor of an Inuit goddess.

Cory: An Inuit goddess? That's interesting. Well, I'm sorry to tell you that the

computers _____ (work).

D Listen. <u>Underline</u> the correct short answer to each question you will hear.

CD1,TR16

1. a. Yes, they are.   b. No, they aren't.
2. a. Yes, she is.   b. No, she's not.
3. a. Yes, he does.   b. No, he doesn't.
4. a. They're using Eskimo.   b. They're using both names.
5. a. Yes, he is.   b. No, he isn't.
6. a. Yes, she is.   b. No, she isn't.

E Look at the picture. Use the verbs in parentheses in the present progressive.

1. (space station / orbit / Earth) *The space station is orbiting Earth.*

2. (astronauts / do / space walk) _____

3. (wings / not work) _____

4. (they / not sit / space station) _____

5. (they / float / space) _____

6. (one astronaut / fix / wing) _____

7. (he / use / special tools) _____

■ **C O M M U N I C A T E**

F **PAIR WORK** Ask and answer questions about the picture in exercise E. Use *yes/no* present progressive questions.

Is the space station orbiting Earth?

Yes, it is.

G **WRITE** Think of yourself, your family members, and your friends. What are they doing today? In your journal, write affirmative and negative sentences. Use the present progressive.

■ GRAMMAR IN CONTENT

A Read and listen.

CD1,TR17

Looking for Aliens

Cindy: Hey, Jim! **What are you doing?**

Jim: I'm looking for aliens.

Cindy: Aliens! **How are you looking for aliens?**

Jim: I'm using a computer program called SETI. SETI stands for the Search for Extraterrestrial Intelligence.

Cindy: Sounds interesting. **What is your computer doing now?**

Jim: It's listening to data from all the radio telescopes in the world. It is looking for aliens. At the same time it's sending the data to a supercomputer in California.

Cindy: **How many people are using the SETI program?**

Jim: Hundreds of people all around the world are using SETI at the moment.

Cindy: Wow! Oh, no! Look at the time.

Jim: **Where are you going?**

Cindy: I'm running to my lecture. I'm late.

data: information

B Check (✔) *True* or *False*.

	True	False
1. Jim is looking for aliens.	☐	☐
2. Jim's computer is listening to data coming from radio telescopes.	☐	☐
3. A computer in California receives data from hundreds of computers.	☐	☐
4. Cindy doesn't know how late it is.	☐	☐

Present Progressive: Information Questions

	Be	Subject	Verb + *-ing*
Who	am	I	talking to?
What	are	you	looking for?
		we	
		they	
Where	is	he	looking for aliens?
Why		she	
How		it	

Note:

Put the *wh-* word or the *how* phrase in front of a question in the present progressive.

Examples: ***Are** aliens visiting us from outer space? **Why** are aliens visiting us from outer space?*

C Complete the questions. Use the correct *wh-* words or *how* phrases and the words in parentheses. Look at the answers to help you.

Alexi: Hello?

Kyung: Hi, Alexi! It's Kyung.

Alexi: Hey! (where / you / call from)

_____Where are you calling from_____?
(1)

Kyung: Home. I'm sitting on the floor.

Alexi: What? (why / you / sit /on the floor) _____?
(2)

Kyung: I'm watching a UFO.

Alexi: You're kidding! (what / the UFO / do) _____?
(3)

Kyung: It's flying outside. It looks really big. It's coming down.

Alexi: It is? And (what / happen / now) _____?
(4)

Kyung: The door of the UFO is opening!

Alexi: Wow! (who / come out) _____?
(5)

Kyung: Aliens! They're small and green.

Alexi: Really? (what / they / do) _____?
(6)

Kyung: They're destroying Earth with laser guns.

Alexi: What? Are you kidding me?

Kyung: Yes, I am.

Alexi: Tell the truth. (what / happening) _____?
(7)

Kyung: I'm watching a science fiction movie on TV.

D Look at the pictures. Use the words in parentheses to write information questions about the pictures. Ask a classmate to write answers to your questions.

1. **Q:** (What) _____What is he looking at_____?

   A: _____

2. **Q:** (What) _____?

   A: _____

3. **Q:** (Where) _____?

  A: _____

4. **Q:** (Who) _____?

  A: _____

5. **Q:** (What) _____?

  A: _____

6. **Q:** (Why) _____?

  A: _____

7. **Q:** (How many) _____?

  A: _____

8. **Q:** (Where) _____?

  A: _____

■ C O M M U N I C A T E

E **PAIR WORK** Work with a classmate. Study the picture. Then close your books. What can you remember? Take turns asking present progressive information questions about the picture.

GRAMMAR AND VOCABULARY Work with a classmate. One student looks at the picture below of astronauts on the moon. The other student looks at the picture on page 236. Ask each other *yes/no* and information questions and answer the questions. Use vocabulary and grammar from this lesson.

PROJECT Prepare a TV news report.

1. Work in small groups.
2. Imagine an alien arrives in your town or city. You are reporters for a local TV news station. Prepare a "live" news story describing what's happening.
3. Present your news report to your class.

 INTERNET Do a search on the Web for Sedna, SETI, UFOs (unidentified flying objects), or aliens. Find some information that is new for you. Tell the class what you have found.

PART 1
The Present Progressive Tense
vs. the Simple Present Tense

PART 2
Stative Verbs

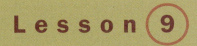

L e s s o n 9

Earth Science: Forestry

■ CONTENT VOCABULARY

Look at the pictures. Do you know the words?

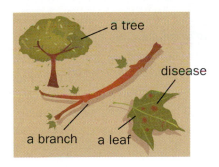

a tree

disease

a branch   a leaf

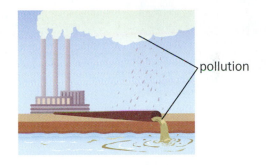

pollution

loggers   protesters

STO Save ve
STO the e
STO Trees rees
STO

to cut down

a ranger

Write the new words in your vocabulary journal.

■ THINK ABOUT IT

Are the world's forests in trouble? Why? Discuss these questions with your class.

■ GRAMMAR IN CONTENT

A Read and listen.

CD1, TR18

carbon dioxide: (CO₂) a gas with no color, taste, or smell produced by burning fossil fuels

The U.S. Forest Service

Reporter: You **work** for the U.S. Forest Service. What **do** you **do?**

Ranger: I'm a forest ranger. I work at Acadia National Park. I **protect** the trees and animals in the forest. I also **look after** visitors to the forests.

Reporter: What **are** you **doing** with that tree?

Ranger: I'**m cutting down** some branches. It has a disease.

Reporter: **Are** diseases **damaging** forests?

Ranger: Yes, they are. Insects, such as the elm bark beetle, **are causing** problems too.

Reporter: Is it true that loggers **are damaging** the forests?

Ranger: Yes, it is. Some loggers **are cutting down** too many trees. They **cut down** more and more trees every year.

Reporter: Why **do** you **think** forests are important?

Ranger: Forests help the earth stay healthy. Trees **take** carbon dioxide out of our air and **put** oxygen into it. Forests **produce** plants that we can use for future medicines. We really need our forests.

B Check (✔) *True* or *False.*

	True	False
1. People are cutting down too many trees in our forests.	☐	☐
2. The main reason to save forests is that they are beautiful.	☐	☐
3. People in forestry are trying to save the forests.	☐	☐
4. Trees and plants produce carbon dioxide and medicines.	☐	☐

Use the simple present:

• for facts. Example: *Forests **produce** medicinal plants.*

• when talking about habits and routines. Example: *Every day I **check** the trees for disease.*

For questions use **Do** or **Does** before the subject. Example: ***Do** forest rangers do an important job?*

Use the present progressive:

• for things that are happening now. Example: *You **are reading** this sentence.*

• for temporary situations, not all the time. Example: *My sister **is working** for the U.S. Forest Service this summer.*

For questions use **Am, Is,** or **Are** before the subject. Example: *Are you applying for a job with the Forest Service?*

C (Circle) the correct verb form.

1. Elm trees (grow / are growing) in forests in America and in parts of Europe.
2. Elm bark beetles (do not live / are not living) in elm trees.
3. Right now the beetle (makes / is making) a hole in the elm tree.
4. Why (does it do / is it doing) this? It (finds / is finding) a place to lay its eggs.
5. Every summer, the beetle (lays / is laying) its eggs in an elm tree.
6. It (does not lay / is not laying) its eggs in other kinds of trees.
7. Sometimes, the beetles (kill / are killing) the tree because they (carry / are carrying) diseases.
8. In late summer, forest rangers (clear / are clearing) dead elm trees from the forest.

D Use the verbs in parentheses to complete these sentences. Decide if you need the simple present or present progressive.

We Must Protect Our Forests

Like a rich man __protects__ (protect) his
      (1)
money, we must protect the forests. I think

that governments _____ (not, protect)
         (2)
our forests. Right now, loggers _____
         (3)
(cut down) trees and _____ (clear) the
        (4)
forests. Why _____ (do) they _____
      (5)   **(6)**
(do) this? Because people _____ (want) to
        (7)
use the wood and they _____ (use) the
        (8)
land.

Forests are important. Trees _____
        (9)
(take) carbon dioxide out of our air and

_____ (put) oxygen into it. Many forests
  (10)

_____ (have) plants that we can use for
  (11)
future medicines. Drug companies_____
               (12)
(produce) new medicines from those plants right

now.

The director of the U.S. Forest Service

_____ (have) an office in Washington, D.C.,
  (13)
but today he _____ (not, work) in his
       (14)
office. He _____ (visit) a forest in Oregon.
       (15)
I _____(hope) he has a plan to protect
  (16)
our forests.

E Correct the errors in each conversation.

1. **A:** What are you ~~do~~ _doing_ in this lesson?

    B: We learn a little about forestry.

2. **A:** Does the United Nations protecting the forests?

    B: Yes, it's.

3. **A:** Is paper coming from trees?

    B: Yes, it's does.

4. **A:** What the problem?

    B: The park is closed today. It snowing.

5. **A:** Where you calling from?

    B: I call from the forest. It's beautiful here.

▪ C O M M U N I C A T E

F PAIR WORK Look at the picture. What's happening? Talk with a classmate.

G WRITE Imagine you are camping in a forest. Write a letter to a friend about it. What are you doing? What can you see? How's the weather? How do you feel?

■ GRAMMAR IN CONTENT

A Read the passage.

CD1,TR19

Forestry

Forestry is about trees. It's also about wildlife. In many places, wildlife **is having** a difficult time. This is because many people take or pollute the animals' land, food, and water. That's why we**'re hearing** that more and more animals are becoming extinct. In a few forests, you **don't hear** birds singing. Some forests **have** almost no animals. There are many animals on the endangered species list.

Forest services **think** they can stop many extinctions. The U.S. Forest Service **is thinking** of more ways to help eagles, bears, and wolves. People **don't see** them often enough. These animals are endangered, but their future is brighter. Forest services **are seeing** more citizens interested in protecting endangered wildlife.

B Check (✔) *True* or *False*.

	True	False
1. Dogs and cats are wild animals.	☐	☐
2. It's hard for some animals because they don't have enough land to live on.	☐	☐
3. Wolves are still endangered.	☐	☐
4. Forestry is not working to help wildlife.	☐	☐
5. More people than ever before are interested in wildlife.	☐	☐

Stative Verbs

Emotions	like, love, hate
Senses	hear, see, smell, taste, feel
States	think, know, believe, understand, need, want
Other	have, cost, weigh

Note:

Stative verbs usually do not talk about actions. We don't usually use these words in the present progressive. Example: *I like soccer.* NOT ~~I am liking soccer.~~

Stative Verbs That Can Be Used in the Present Progressive

Verb	Examples
Feel	We **feel** that forests are very important. (feel = believe) We're **feeling** good about the future of the forests. (feel = experience)
Have	This government **has** a forest service. (have = own) The ranchers **are having** a meeting. (have = do)
Hear	He doesn't **hear** those bird calls. I don't know why not. (hear = use the ears) We're **hearing** strange stories about a creature in the forest. (hear = witness)
See	I **see** an eagle high up in that tree. It's beautiful! (see = use the eyes) They're **seeing** the forests get smaller and smaller. (see = witness) Nancy **is seeing** Ken. (see = to date)
Smell	I **smell** something burning. (involuntary act) "What are you doing?" "I'm **smelling** these flowers." (voluntary act)
Taste	I **taste** strawberry flavor in this drink. (involuntary act) "What is the chef doing?" "She's **tasting** the soup." (voluntary act)
Think	Kim **thinks** we can save the forests. (think = believe) Please be quiet! I'm **thinking**. (think = use the brain to create, imagine, remember)

Note:

Some stative verbs can take the progressive form. The difference between these two forms is meaning, not time.

C **Circle** the best form of each verb for the sentence.

1. I (am thinking / (think)) that forestry is very interesting.
2. (Are you seeing / Do you see) anybody these days? I know you like George.
3. The Forest Service (is having / has) a large number of forest rangers in the national parks.
4. We (aren't feeling / don't feel) that lions are an endangered species.
5. "What (are you doing / do you do), Ms. Randall?" "I'm a forest ranger in Florida."
6. Universities (are seeing / see) more students registering for forestry courses.
7. "How's the Canadian population of polar bears?" "It (isn't doing / doesn't do) very well."

D **Look at each picture. Complete the sentences about each picture. Use the verb in parentheses.**

1. The hunter _____ (feel) for his gun.

   He _____ (not, feel) it's important
   to protect wolves.

2. The tourist _____ (smell) the flowers, but they

   _____ (smell) terrible.

3. Keisha _____ (think) about bald eagles. She

   _____ (thinks) eagles are beautiful.

4. **Reporter:** I see lots of protesters here. Why are
   they here?

   Protester: We _____ (see) the destruction of the

   forests. We _____ (not, like) it. We

   _____ (want) to stop the destruction.

5. **Reporter:** "Mr. President, what are you doing
   about the forests?"

   President: "Well, I _____ (have) a new report
   from the Forest Service. The Service

   _____ (have) a meeting right now

   about the forests. I _____ (love) the

   forests and I _____ (hear) a lot

   about the problems. But we _____
   (need) more information about the damage to
   our forests."

E **WRITE** In your notebook, write a short paragraph about your thoughts on the environment. Use stative verbs in the simple present or present progressive when possible.

> We are seeing more and more interest these days in forestry. People feel that it is important to protect our forests and our wildlife. I think this is very important, too.
>
> My friends and I are thinking about a trip to one of the national parks. We would like to see a beautiful, natural place.

Connection | Putting It Together

GRAMMAR AND VOCABULARY Interview classmates. Find out one thing that each classmate does or doesn't do regularly and one thing they are doing or not doing today. Use the grammar and vocabulary from the lesson.

PROJECT Prepare a report about a forest or natural habitat.

- Work in small groups. Choose a forest or other natural habitat that you know.
- Go to the library or the Web site. Find information about the dangers to the forest or natural area. What's happening to the forest? Are people polluting the rivers?
- Write a short report about what you found out. Include photos if you want.
- Present your report to the class.
- Be prepared to answer questions from your classmates.

 INTERNET Go online. Use the keywords "endangered species list" to find which animals are endangered. Take notes on one that interests you and report to your class.

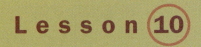
Business: Processes and Procedures

■ CONTENT VOCABULARY

Look at the pictures. Do you know the words?

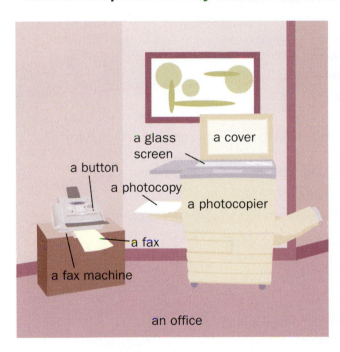

a glass screen

a cover

a button

a photocopy

a photocopier

a fax

a fax machine

an office

colleagues

a folder

Write the new words in your vocabulary journal.

■ THINK ABOUT IT

Do you know someone who works in an office? What do they do? Discuss with the class.

■ GRAMMAR IN CONTENT

CD1,TR20

A Read and listen to the following conversation between two office workers.

> **Making a Photocopy**
>
> **Antonio:** Hi, Shi-Mae. I'd like to ask a favor. Can you show me how to make a photocopy?
>
> **Shi-Mae:** Sure, Antonio. It's really easy. **First,** turn on the photocopier if it's off. **Then** lift the cover and put the memo face down on this glass plate.
>
> **Antonio:** Okay.
>
> **Shi-Mae:** **Next,** put the cover down and press this button to choose the number of copies you want.
>
> **Antonio:** Then what?
>
> **Shi-Mae:** **After that,** just press "Start."
>
> **Antonio:** All right.
>
> **Shi-Mae:** **Finally,** don't forget to take back your original and turn off the photocopier.
>
> **Antonio:** Okay, Shi-Mae. I can do that. Thanks for the lesson!
>
> **Shi-Mae:** You're welcome, Antonio.

favor: a helpful act   **original:** not a copy; the first

B Check (✔) *True* or *False.*

	True	False
1. Antonio has more experience with photocopiers than Shi-Mae.	☐	☐
2. Shi-Mae knows how to make a photocopy.	☐	☐
3. Antonio knows exactly how to make a photocopy.	☐	☐
4. Antonio told Shi-Mae why he wants to make those photocopies.	☐	☐
5. Shi-Mae said that Antonio should leave the machine on.	☐	☐

Time Sequence Markers	
First **Then** **Next** **After that** **Finally**	**Notes:** • Time sequence markers describe the steps someone needs to take to do something. A step is each action that someone needs to do in a process. • Begin with *First* and end with *Finally. Then, next, after that* do not have to stay in order.

C Below is a list of steps to send an e-mail. Write a number on the blank before each step to show what to do first, second, etc.

___ Click on "New" to type a new e-mail message.

___ Click on the large text box and type your message.

_1_ Login to your e-mail.

___ Click on "Send."

___ Type e-mail address(es) in the "To" box.

___ Type the reason for the e-mail in the "Subject" box.

___ Type in your user name and password, and click on "Okay."

___ Proofread your message and make corrections or changes.

___ Type more e-mail addresses in the "Cc" box to send others a copy.

D Use time sequence markers to write the steps from exercise C.

How to Send an E-mail

First, login to your e-mail.

_____

_____

_____

_____

_____

_____

_____

■ COMMUNICATE

E **WRITE** Choose one activity from the list or think of something else. In your notebook, write the necessary steps to do this activity.

- how to plan a staff meeting
- how to plan a conference call
- how to create folders for new accounts and file them
- how to make a pot of coffee

■ GRAMMAR IN CONTENT

CD1,TR21

A Read and listen to the following conversation that three office workers are having.

Where Are My Papers?

Neil: What's up, Paul?

Paul: I can't find some important papers. I put them **on** the desk, but they're gone.

Neil: Maybe you put them **in** one of the drawers. Did you check?

Paul: They're locked. The key's not here. Somebody took the key **out**!

Neil: Someone took your key **out of** the drawer?

Paul: Yes! And maybe somebody took those papers **off of** my desk, too. What's happening? Wait a minute. There's Gina. Maybe somebody came **into** this office and she saw the person. Hey, Gina! Can I talk to you for a minute?

Gina: Sure, Paul. What's up?

Paul: Did anybody come **into** my office this afternoon?

Gina: A few people walked **past** your office, but nobody went **in**.

Paul: I don't know what's happening, but I really hate a mystery!

what's up?: what's happening?   **gone:** missing, disappeared

B Check (✔) *True* or *False*.

	True	False
1. This conversation takes place in Gina's office.	☐	☐
2. Paul is upset because he can't find his key.	☐	☐
3. Neil thinks somebody came into the office and took those papers.	☐	☐
4. Gina comes into the office to find out what is wrong.	☐	☐
5. Gina cannot help the two men solve the mystery.	☐	☐

He is coming **into** the office.
He's going **through** the door.

He is putting the memo **on (to)** the desk.

He is coming **out of** the office.

The memo is falling **off (of)** the desk.

She is walking **along** the corridor.

She is walking **by / past** the photocopier.

She's walking **down** the stairs.
He's walking **up** the stairs.

He is walking **toward** the fax machine.

Notes:
- For *into*, *onto*, and *off of*, if there is no object, use *in*, *on*, and *off*. Example: *The secretary walked in.* (NOT: *The secretary walked into.*)
- For *out of*, if there is no object, we use only *out*. Example: *She came out.* (NOT: *She came out of.*)
- We use *by* or *past* when a person or thing goes in front of another thing, but does not stop.

C Look at the picture of Hanif's commute to work. Complete the paragraph with the prepositions of location from the box.

through	toward	up	~~along~~	past	out of	into

Hanif has a short commute to work. First, he drives _____*along*_____ a river. Then, he goes _____ a hospital. Next, he goes _____ a short tunnel. When he comes _____ the tunnel, he goes _____ a hill. Next, he drives _____ the office building and goes _____ the parking garage. His commute takes 15 minutes.

D Write sentences about the pictures using prepositions of movement.

1. **Q:** What's Ivanna doing?

   A: _____*She's getting out of her chair.*_____

2. **Q:** Where is she walking?

   A: _____

3. **Q:** Where is she putting the fax?

   A: _____

4. **Q:** What's the fax doing?

   A: _____

5. **Q:** Where's the fax falling?

   A: _____

6. **Q:** What's she doing now?

   A: _____

■ COMMUNICATE

E **PAIR WORK** Tell a partner about how you get to school or work. Use prepositions of movement.

GRAMMAR AND VOCABULARY Work with a classmate. You're the boss of a small company. You're having a holiday party for your office staff at your home. Tell your colleague how to get to your home. Use the grammar and vocabulary from the lesson.

PROJECT Do a silent demonstration.

1. Work with another classmate.
2. Decide on a demonstration to show the class how to do or make something in an office.
3. Write down all the steps you need to do or make this.
4. Practice the demonstration. Act out the steps.
5. Present your demonstration to the class. Your classmates will guess what you are demonstrating.

 INTERNET How do you normally get on the Internet? What steps do you need to take to get to your favorite website? Write the steps down and tell your classmates.

A **Complete the sentences. Use time sequence markers and prepositions in the blanks.**

How to Mail a Letter

_____(1), write the name and address of where the letter is going _____(2) the center of the front of the envelope. _____(3), write your return address _____(4) the upper left-hand corner. _____(5), take one stamp _____(6) a sheet of stamps and stick it _____(7) the envelope _____(8) the upper right-hand corner. _____(9), put your letter _____(10) the envelope. Before you seal the flap, make sure everything is all right. _____(11), use your tongue to lick the glue, close the flap, and seal it. _____(12), when you pass _____(13) a mailbox, drop the letter _____(14) the box.

B **Complete this conversation with three students. Use pronouns and possessive nouns, possessive adjectives, and possessive pronouns. Use the words in parentheses.**

Kim: Irene, (these books and this book bag/belong) _____(1) to you?

    Are _____(2) _____(3)?

Irene: No, _____(4)'re not _____(5). _____(6)'re (Ben) _____(7).

Kim: Really? (Ben/have) _____(8) a pink book bag? I (think)

    _____(9) _____(10) is pink! _____(11)'m sure _____(12)'s green.

Irene: Okay, well, ask Monica. Maybe _____(13) (belong) _____(14) to her sister,

    Jessica.

Kim: Hey, Monica. Are these books and this book bag (Jessica) _____(15)?

Monica: Well, that book bag is _____(16). _____(17) both (own) _____(18) pink

    book bags. _____(19) (own) _____(20) that dark pink _____(21), but I

    have a light pink _____(22). Oh! Those two books aren't _____(23).

    _____(24)'re _____(25) (brother) _____(26). Thanks for finding

    _____(27)! _____(28)'ll be happy to know _____(29)'re okay.

C **Complete this conversation between two students.**

Luke: Hey, May! Where (you/go) _____ now?
(1)

May: To the cafeteria. I (feel) _____ hungry, so I (want) _____
(2)   (3)

to get some lunch now. Why (you/ask) _____ me?
(4)

(you/want) _____ to get some lunch, too?
(5)

Luke: Yeah, but I (like) _____ the food in the cafeteria. It (taste)
(6)

_____ strange to me and it (smell) _____ strange, too.
(7)   (8)

I (think) _____ the food in Edna's Café is better.
(9)

May: You know, I usually (bring) _____ my lunch to school to save money,
(10)

but this week I (bring) _____ it because I (live) _____
(11)   (12)

at home.

Luke: Why not? (you/have) _____ problems with your parents?
(13)

May: No! Nothing like that! My father (paint) _____ the inside of our
(14)

house. Well, my stomach (talk) _____ to me. Let's go to Edna's.
(15)

LEARNER LOG Check (✔) *Yes* or *I Need More Practice.*

Lesson	I Can Use . . .	Yes	I Need More Practice
6	Possessive Nouns, Adjectives, and Pronouns; *Whose* Questions		
7	Personal Pronouns; *One, Ones, It,* and *They*		
8	The Present Progressive in Statements, *Yes/No* Questions, Short Answers, and Information Questions		
9	Verbs in the Present Progressive Compared to the Simple Present; Stative Verbs		
10	Time Sequence Markers and Prepositions of Movement		

PART 1
General Statements: Ø and *A/An*

PART 2
General and Specific Statements:
Ø and *The*

Lesson (11)

Veterinary Medicine:
Being a Veterinarian

■ CONTENT VOCABULARY

Look at the pictures. Do you know the words?

a clinic

a cat

a canary

a dog

a goldfish

reptiles

a snake   an iguana

Write the new words in your vocabulary journal.

■ THINK ABOUT IT

Do you think having a pet is a good thing? Why or why not? Discuss these questions with your class.

■ **GRAMMAR IN CONTENT**

A **Read and listen.**

CD1,TR22

Becoming a Vet

Many people love **pets.** For them, **life** is better because they have **a pet.** But somebody has to protect **pets** from **disease** and take care of them when they are sick. That job is for a **veterinarian, a "vet."**

Veterinary medicine is a rewarding **career** that requires four years of **study** after **college. A vet** takes care of **dogs** and **cats,** but some vets specialize in the care of **birds** or **reptiles** such as **snakes** and **iguanas. Vets' salaries** are high.

Health is something **humans** need. **Animals** need it, too.

rewarding: satisfying

to specialize: to study and work in a specific subject

General Statements with *Ø* and *A/An*

A dog makes **a** great **pet.** (OR: **Dogs** make great **pets.**)
Life is better with **a pet.**
Health is important for **pets,** too.
I love **dogs.**

Notes:

• Make general statements to describe things that are true.

• In general statements about count nouns, use the singular form of the subject with *a* or *an* or the plural form of the subject with the zero article. The meaning does not change.

• In general statements, don't use articles with uncountable nouns. Use the zero article (*Ø*).

B **Check (✔)** *True* **or** *False.*

	True	False
1. Pets can make life better for people.	☐	☐
2. Veterinary school lasts for four years.	☐	☐
3. Every vet can take care of every kind of animal.	☐	☐
4. Salaries for vets are high.	☐	☐

C Read the following sentences. Decide if they are correct or not. If they are incorrect, make the necessary corrections.

1. *A*
   ^ Veterinarian receives four years of ~~the~~ training.

2. The veterinarians take care of animals, not people.

3. Dog is a person's best friend.

4. Some vets look after the reptiles.

5. Veterinary medicine is a rewarding profession.

6. All animals must have a food and water.

D Add an article in each blank if necessary.

1. (a) _____ schools of (b) _____ veterinary medicine can cost a lot of

   (c) _____ money.

2. (a) _____ veterinary students usually attend (b) _____ four-year
   program.

3. (a) _____ veterinarians love (b) _____ animals and want to keep them

   in (c) _____ good health.

4. Most vets take care of (a) _____ dogs and (b) _____ cats. Some take

   care of (c) _____ unusual pets.

5. Many people have (a) _____ dog for protection. (b) _____ cat can't
   really protect anything.

6. (a) _____ pets offer their human companions (b) _____ love and

   (c) _____ affection.

7. (a) _____ American will pay a lot of (b) _____ money to keep

   (c) _____ pet healthy and happy.

8. (a) _____ vet can work (b) _____ long hours, but this work is very
   rewarding.

■ **C O M M U N I C A T E**

E **PAIR WORK** Work with a classmate. Take turns telling each other about a pet each of you had or still has. Talk about things such as these: What kind of animal *is/was* it? Where *does/did* it live? Where *does/did* it sleep? What *is/was* its favorite toy? *Do/Did* you take it to a vet? Why?

■ GRAMMAR IN CONTENT

CD1, TR23

A Read and listen to the following conversation between Margot, a veterinary assistant, and Dr. Maynard, the vet she works for.

advice: opinion(s) given to someone about what to do

to offer: to present something that a person may or may not accept

---

A Career in the Zoo

Margot: Dr. Maynard, I need some advice.

Dr. Maynard: Sure, Margot. How can I help you?

Margot: I'm in my second year of vet school now, and I have to decide if I want to specialize.

Dr. Maynard: I know you love **animals**, Margot. **The animals** in our clinic always feel that from you. How about staying with **pet care?** I know you enjoy **the pet care** we offer here.

Margot: I think I'm more interested in **wildlife** than in pets. I know that **the wildlife** in our zoos needs **special attention.** I think I'd like to give those animals **the special attention** they require.

Dr. Maynard: **Zoos** are always looking for **good vets**, Margot. I'm sure **the zoos** right here in our city will offer you a good job after you graduate. So go for it!

Margot: Thanks for your advice, Dr. Maynard. I think I will.

B Check (✔) *True* or *False.*

	True	False
1. Margot wants Dr. Maynard's opinion.	☐	☐
2. Margot is ready to graduate from veterinary school.	☐	☐
3. Pets and zoo animals require the same care.	☐	☐
4. Margot thinks she'd like to work at a zoo.	☐	☐

General and Specific Statements	
General	**Specific**
A vet helps sick animals get better. **Students** need to study.	**The vet** made my dog feel better. **The students** in Jim's class study very hard.

Notes:

• General statements are not usually made with *the.*

• Use *the* when making a statement about somebody or something specific.

C Read each of the following sentences. <u>Underline</u> the subject. Then, decide if the subject of each sentence is general or specific. Check the appropriate box.

	General	Specific
1. <u>Proper nutrition for zoo animals</u> is very complicated.	☑	☐
2. Zoo animals need professionals to take care of them.	☐	☐
3. The tigers in our zoo eat fresh meat.	☐	☐
4. Tigers eat fresh meat.	☐	☐
5. Meat is a very good source of protein.	☐	☐
6. The meat our tigers eat is mostly beef.	☐	☐

D Read the following sentences. Decide if they are correct. If they are incorrect, correct them.

1. Dr. Maynard is ⌄*the* veterinarian that Margot works for.

2. Dr. Maynard studied the veterinary medicine at the Florida National University.

3. The veterinary students study for four years in a school of veterinary medicine.

4. After graduation, most new vets work in animal clinics.

5. Dr. Maynard opened two clinics. The names of clinics are Pet Haven North and Pet Haven South.

6. Dr. Maynard likes helping sick and injured animals.

7. Once a year, Dr. Maynard gives the vaccinations to all his dog and cat patients.

8. You can find the real success in the life by helping the people or the animals.

■ **C O M M U N I C A T E**

E **WRITE** Write a short paragraph in your notebook about an animal that you like or a pet that you have.

> Butch is a German shepard dog. Butch loves to play with a ball.
> He always wants me to throw the ball. He runs after it and then
> brings it back to me. I can throw that ball all day, but Butch never
> gets tired of running after it.

GRAMMAR AND VOCABULARY Interview four classmates. Find out which ones have pets. Fill in the chart with the information you collect. Use the grammar and vocabulary in this lesson.

Do you have pets?

Yes, I do. I have two cats. I have a Persian and a Siamese.

Classmate	Kind of Animal	Breed	Sex	Favorite Toy(s)	Where It Sleeps
Gina	cats	a Persian and a Siamese	female	balls	one in a small cat bed, the other on the couch in the living room

 INTERNET PROJECT Work with three or four classmates. Do the following:

1. Go online. Search for schools of veterinary medicine.
2. Find out . . .
   - the requirements for entering the school
   - the different programs the school offers
   - specializations in veterinary medicine
   - any information about jobs after graduation
3. Present your information to the class. Let each person in your group present one of these topics.

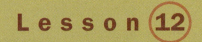
Health Science: Dietetics

■ CONTENT VOCABULARY

Look at the pictures. Do you know the words?

vitamins, minerals

fat, calories

protein

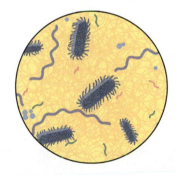

bacteria

Write the new words in your vocabulary journal.

■ THINK ABOUT IT

What foods are good for you? Do you eat healthy food? What are the dangers of bacteria? Discuss your answers with your class.

■ GRAMMAR IN CONTENT

A Read and listen.

CD1,TR24

Dietetics

Fifty years ago, **many** people knew that foods with **a lot of** fat were not good for us, but **few** people knew there were good fats and bad fats. At that time, we knew that vitamins and minerals were good for us, but doctors had **little** information about antioxidants, nutrients that can help fight cancer.

The field of dietetics is helping to change that situation. In recent times, dieticians and researchers discovered **lots of** important facts about nutrients. Nutrients keep our bodies healthy, protect us from diseases, and help slow the effects of getting older.

A few scientists say that good nutrition can help us live **much** longer than we do now. Dietetics is **much** more important today than it was fifty years ago, and it will be even more important in the future.

a nutrient: any of the substances contained in food that are essential to life

a field: an area of activity, interest, or study

B Check (✔) *True* or *False.*

	True	False
1. Antioxidants help people fight cancer.	☐	☐
2. Doctors know nothing about antioxidants.	☐	☐
3. Dieticians are people who are on a diet.	☐	☐
4. Good nutrition can help us live healthy, long lives.	☐	☐

Quantifiers with Uncountable Nouns

Quantifiers	Meaning	Examples
a lot of/lots of	a large quantity	It's good to drink **a lot of water**.
much	(use **much** usually in negative statements)	There isn't **much nutrition** in lettuce.
a little	a small quantity	He always puts **a little salt** on his food.
little	a small quantity (with a negative meaning)	There is **little nutrition** in lettuce.

Quantifiers with Countable Nouns

Quantifiers	Meaning	Examples
many a lot of/lots of	a large amount	We get **many** nutrients from vegetables. We get **lots of** nutrients from vegetables.
a few some	a small quantity	There are only **a few** calories in spinach.
few	a small quantity (with a negative meaning)	**Few** people know about good nutrition.
any	no amount if the verb before it is negative	There aren't **any** carrots in this soup.

C (Circle) the quantifier that best completes each sentence.

1. There's (much / **a lot of**) protein in beans.
2. (Many / Much) vegetables contain antioxidants.
3. It is good to have (a little / any) fat in your diet.
4. (Lot of / Lots of) colleges now offer degrees in dietetics.
5. She drinks (few / a few) glasses of water each day because it is healthy.
6. In the past, (few / a little) doctors knew how important nutrition was.
7. Can I have (a few / a little) cherries, please?

D Look at the nutrition facts for ice cream and beans. Complete the sentences about them by using the quantifiers in the box below. You can use a quantifier more than one time.

many	much	a lot of	a few	few	a little	little

Refried Beans
Serving Size 1 cup (130g)
Servings Per Container about 3.5

Amount Per Serving

Calories 120   Calories from Fat 10

                           % Daily Value*

Total Fat 1g	2%
Saturated Fat 0g	0%
Cholesterol 0mg	0%
Sodium 610mg	25%
Total Carbohydrate 20g	7%
Dietary Fiber 6g	24%
Sugars 1g	
Protein 7g	

Vitamin A 0%	•	Vitamin C 0%
Calcium 2%	•	Iron 15%

Vanilla Ice Cream
Serving Size 1 cup (106g)
Servings Per Container 4

Amount Per Serving

Calories 270   Calories from Fat 160

                           % Daily Value*

Total Fat 18g	28%
Saturated Fat 11g	55%
Cholesterol 120mg	40%
Sodium 70mg	3%
Total Carbohydrate 21g	7%
Dietary Fiber 0g	0%
Sugars 21g	
Protein 5g	

Vitamin A 15%	•	Vitamin C 0%
Calcium 15%	•	Iron 0%

1. There aren't _many / a lot of_ servings in these containers.

2. The ice cream has _____ calories for this small serving.

3. A healthy person needs about 70 grams of protein per day. There isn't _____ protein in these servings.

4. The ice cream has 18 grams of fat, but the refried beans have just _____ fat.

5. Compared to the ice cream, there are _____ sugars in the refried beans.

6. Compared to the refried beans, there's _____ fat in the ice cream.

7. There's _____ calcium in the refried beans.

8. Compared to the ice cream, there are _____ milligrams of sodium in the refried beans.

9. The ice cream has no dietary fiber, but the refried beans have _____ grams.

■ COMMUNICATE

E PAIR WORK Interview a classmate. Find out what he or she usually eats and drinks on a typical weekday. Complete the chart.

Breakfast	Snack	Lunch	Snack	Dinner

F WRITE Use the information your classmate gave you in exercise E to write a description of his/her eating habits. Use quantifiers in your description.

GRAMMAR IN CONTENT

CD1,TR25

A Read and listen to this conversation between Ms. Hach, a career counselor, and Toni, a student who isn't sure about a career.

A Career Choice

Ms. Hach: So, what can I do for you today, Toni?

Toni: I can't decide what to do after I graduate. There are **too many** choices.

Ms. Hach: Is there a career that interests you?

Toni: Well, maybe something with food. I enjoy cooking and planning menus.

Ms. Hach: Okay. Would you like to be a chef? Or are you interested in dietetics?

Toni: Hmm . . . Dietetics. That field includes food service, right?

Ms. Hach: It includes nutrition and food service. Dieticians also know about bacteria and disease control. There are **too few** qualified people in the food service industry and in food control. **Too many** people think that dietetics is only about nutrition, but it's also about those other important areas. There's **too little** information about these career opportunities in the school library, so I'll get some brochures and give them to you. It's a growing field.

Toni: Thanks, Ms. Hach. That sounds good.

to graduate: to receive a diploma or degree from a school

a counselor: an adviser

qualified: meets the requirements

B Check (✔) *True* or *False*.

	True	False
1. Toni is sure about her career plans.	☐	☐
2. Ms. Hach thinks Toni can be a great chef.	☐	☐
3. Ms. Hach tells Toni that the food service industry needs more qualified people.	☐	☐
4. Ms. Hach tells Toni to look for information in the school library.	☐	☐
5. Toni seems interested in a career in dietetics.	☐	☐

Quantifiers with *too*

Quantifiers	Meaning	Examples
too many	more than is good; more than is necessary; with countable nouns	There are **too many calories** in this pie, so I'll have the fresh fruit.
too few	not enough; less than is good; less than is necessary; with countable nouns	**Too few doctors** learn about nutrition in medical school.
too much	more than is good; more than is necessary; with uncountable nouns	People eat **too much fast food.**
too little	not enough; less than is good; less than is necessary; with uncountable nouns	Adults with **too little insulin** suffer from diabetes.

Note:

The word *too* is negative; something is not good. Don't confuse *too much* with *much* or *a lot of.* Example: *She has* **too much** *work.* (She's always tired. She never relaxes. It's a bad thing.) *She has* **a lot of** *work.* (This doesn't tell us that it's a bad thing. It can be good.)

C Look at these pictures. Write a sentence that describes each picture. Use *too many, too few, too much,* or *too little.*

1. The restaurant closed because there were _____*too few*_____ customers.

2. He is eating _____ doughnuts.

3. She has _____ water.

4. There are _____ salads.

5. There are _____ coffee cups.

D Read the e-mail from Janet. Fill in each blank with *too many, too few, too much,* or *too little.*

Hi, Pavel! How are you doing?

Bad news. I just quit my job. Restaurant servers make _____*too little*_____ money. I'm now going
                                                        (1)

to college. I'm taking courses in the food service industry. I don't have a lot of time for fun because

I'm taking _____ courses at the same time. I'm always tired because I have
                    (2)

_____ schoolwork.
          (3)

My accounting class has 38 students in it. The instructor can't give me much attention because

there are _____ students in the class. Only seven students are in my nutrition class
                (4)

this semester. That worries the school's director. The director thinks that _____
                                                                                    (5)

students are interested in good nutrition. One of my friends was interested in the program, but

decided it was too difficult. There's _____ coursework.
                                              (6)

■ **C O M M U N I C A T E**

E **PAIR WORK** Tell a classmate at least four complaints that you have about your
family, friends, neighborhood, job, school, etc. Use *too many, too few, too much,*
and *too little.* Let your classmate tell you at least four complaints.

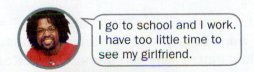

I go to school and I work.
I have too little time to
see my girlfriend.

F WRITE Write a paragraph about the complaints that your classmate told you in exercise E.

Connection | Putting It Together

GRAMMAR AND VOCABULARY Work with a partner. Talk about the food in the pictures. Which foods do you like to eat a lot of? Which foods have a lot of fat? Which foods are high in calories? Which foods do you eat too little of? Use the grammar and vocabulary from the lesson.

PROJECT Write a report on food nutrition.

1. Work in small groups.
2. Choose a food that all of you like and eat often. Bring a container of that food into class. It can be a can, a box, or a plastic bag. Study the nutrition label and find out the following:

   • Which items on the label are good for you? Why are they good for you?
   • Which items on the label are bad for you? Why are they bad for you?
   • Is the amount of each item okay for you, or is it a problem?

3. Use the Internet, if you have to, to find out the answers to the questions above.
4. Write a report about the food you are investigating.
5. Present your report to the class.

 INTERNET Go online. Use the keywords "online," "shopping," and "food" to find online supermarkets. Imagine you want to buy food for dinner. Choose items for your dinner that are healthy. Tell your classmates why you chose these items.

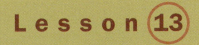
Agriculture: Modern Farming

■ CONTENT VOCABULARY

Look at the pictures. Do you know the words?

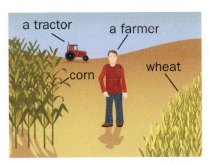

a tractor   a farmer

corn   wheat

crops

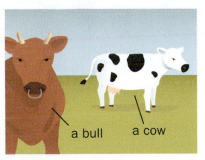

a bull   a cow

cattle

a turkey

a chicken

poultry

Killer   Granules   spray

pesticides

Write the new words in your vocabulary journal.

■ THINK ABOUT IT

Are there farms near where you live? What crops do they grow? Do they have cattle or poultry? Are the farms big or small? Discuss these questions with your classmates.

■ GRAMMAR IN CONTENT

CD1,TR26

A Read and listen.

GM Foods

In 2003, there were about 170 million acres of genetically modified (GM) crops in 18 countries. What are GM crops? GM crops are plants changed by humans. Foods from GM crops are often **bigger than** foods from traditional crops.

Why are farmers growing GM crops? Some farmers think GM crops are **safer than** traditional crops. They think growing GM crops is **easier than** growing traditional crops because they don't need to use pesticides.

Some consumers think that GM crops will be **more expensive than** traditional crops. They think that GM foods are **healthier** because they don't go bad very fast. Many others think that foods from GM crops are not safe.

an acre: a piece of land measuring 4,840 square yards

B Check (✔) *True* or *False.*

	True	False
1. GM crops are the same as regular crops.	☐	☐
2. Some farmers think growing GM crops is easy.	☐	☐
3. Everyone thinks food from GM crops is safe.	☐	☐

Regular Comparative Adjectives		
Adjective Type	**Notes**	**Examples**
one syllable	Add *-er* or *-r* and put the word *than* after it.	
	• For adjectives with one vowel and one final consonant, double the final consonant and add *-er.*	big, bigger/hot, hotter
	• For adjectives with two vowels, add *-er.*	cool, cooler/great, greater
	• For adjectives with two consonants, add *-er.*	cold, colder/fast, faster
	• For adjectives ending in *-e,* add *-r.*	nice, nicer/large, larger
two syllables ending in *-y*	Change *-y* to *-i* and add *-ier* and put the word *than* after it.	healthy, health**ier**

Regular Comparative Adjectives

Adjective Type	Notes	Examples
some two-syllable adjectives	Add *-er/-ier* OR use *more* before the adjective and the word *than* after it.	
	• Some two-syllable adjectives that you can compare in two ways are *angry, clever, common, friendly, gentle, handsome, narrow, quiet,* and *simple.*	friendly, more friendly, friendly, friendlier than
	• Put *less* before the adjective and the word *than* after it.	not friendly, less friendly than
three or more syllables	Put *more* or *less* before the adjective and the word *than* after it.	expensive, more expensive than
		Nonorganic foods are **less** perishable **than** organic foods.

C Complete the dialogue with the verbs and adjectives in parentheses. Make comparative forms of adjectives and use the word *than.*

Kyle: Do you know which college you want to go to next year?

Betty: Yes. I want to go to Texas A&M University.

Kyle: A&M? Why?

Betty: I looked at many schools, but A&M offers ___*more exciting*___ **(1)** (exciting) courses _____ the others. Their curriculum is _____ **(2)** (hard) _____ some other schools, but the school is also _____ **(3)** (famous) _____ many other colleges.

Kyle: Do you plan on being a farmer?

Betty: Yes, I do. I'm _____ **(4)** (interested) in feeding people _____ in any other career. And I think a career in agriculture will be _____ **(5)** (stressful) _____ a career in high finance and business. I know that's what *you* like.

Kyle: I really think that farming is _____ **(6)** (stressful) _____ business.

D Write sentences to compare the pictures. Use comparatives of the adjectives in parentheses.

1. (fat) _Cow A is fatter than cow B._

2. (healthy) _____

_____

3. (heavy) _____

_____

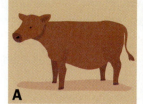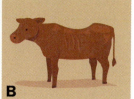

A   B

4. (big) _____

_____

5. (modern) _____

_____

6. (beautiful) _____

_____

A   B

7. (tall) _____

_____

8. (tasty) _____

_____

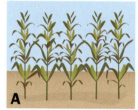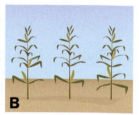

A   B

■ COMMUNICATE

E **PAIR WORK** Compare these two farmers. Use the adjectives in the box.

Clem   Judd

| old   tall   thin   curly   friendly   long |
| short   practical   dangerous |

F **PAIR WORK** Compare yourself to your partner. Discuss what's different and the same about you.

■ GRAMMAR IN CONTENT

A Read the dialogue.

CD1, TR27

Organic Vegetables

Liam: Hey, Lynn! I see you're shopping for groceries, too.

Lynn: Hi, Liam. Look at these organic tomatoes! Aren't they beautiful?

Liam: Organic? I can't afford organic.

Lynn: They are expensive. But organic vegetables are much **better than** nonorganic vegetables. Farmers use **fewer** chemicals to grow them so they're healthier.

Liam: Yeah, I know organic farms use **fewer** pesticides **than** nonorganic farms. But organic vegetables are still more expensive **than** regular ones.

Lynn: Well, eating organic vegetables is **better than** eating nonorganic vegetables. But not eating any vegetables is **worse**.

afford: to be able to pay for something without difficulty

B Check (✔) *True* or *False*.

	True	False
1. Liam thinks organic food is expensive.	☐	☐
2. Lynn thinks organic food isn't healthy.	☐	☐
3. Lynn thinks eating vegetables is bad.	☐	☐

Irregular Comparative Adjectives		
Irregular Adjectives	**Comparative Phrases**	**Examples**
good	better than	Organic potatoes are **better than** nonorganic potatoes.
bad	worse than	For crops, drought is **worse than** insects.
far	farther than	A tractor goes **farther than** a horse and cart.

Note:

It is also acceptable to use *further than*.

Irregular Comparative Adjectives with Nouns

Irregular Adjectives		Comparative Adjectives	Countable Nouns	*than*	
a few a lot of	Ashley's farm has	fewer more	cows crops	than	mine.

		Comparative Adjectives	Uncountable Nouns	*than*	
a little much	Ashley's farm has	less more	cattle corn	than	mine.

C Complete the sentences about the pictures. Use irregular comparative adjectives.

Reiko   Roberto

1. Reiko has a lot of corn, <u>but Roberto has more</u> <u>corn than Reiko.</u>

Roberto   Philip

2. Roberto has many sheep, but _____ _____.

3. Harvey's apples are good, but _____ _____.

4. Marvin's apples have a lot of flavor, but _____.

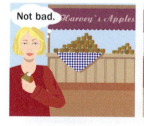

Welcome to
Orchardville
population: 1,518

Farmington   17 miles
Sunnyvale Farm   8 miles
Shadylane Farm 11 miles

5. Farmington has 4,382 people in it. Orchardville _____.

6. Shadylane Farm is _____ from Orchardville _____ Sunnyvale Farm is.

D Look at the chart. Write sentences comparing the two farms. Use irregular comparative adjectives.

Farming Industry Report: Poultry		
	Sunnyvale Farm	Shadylane Farm
1. Profit	$100,000	$560,000
2. Employees	50	105
3. Chickens	3,500	10,500
4. Turkeys	2,100	1,650
5. States they sell to	3	10

1. _____ Sunnyvale farm makes less profit than Shadylane farm. _____

2. _____

3. _____

4. _____

5. _____

■ COMMUNICATE

E **WRITE** Write a paragraph comparing organic food and nonorganic food. Use irregular comparative adjectives.

F **GROUP WORK** Compare two places you know well. Use the words in the box to help. Discuss your comparisons with a small group.

population food weather people history agriculture cities economy

Chile has fewer people than the United States and the cities are smaller.

GRAMMAR AND VOCABULARY Work with a classmate. Spot the eight differences between the two pictures. Use the grammar and vocabulary from the lesson.

PROJECT Debate agricultural issues.

1. Work in groups. Divide into two teams.
2. Choose one of these topics to debate:
   - Chemicals are bad for farms.
   - Organically grown crops are healthier for us.
   - Bigger farms are better than smaller farms.
3. One team will be "pro" (meaning "for" something). The other team will be "con" (meaning "against" something). Prepare comparative statements to defend your team's opinion, pro or con.
4. Have a debate.

 INTERNET Go online. Choose a country you want to know more about. Compare that country's agriculture to the agriculture in your country. How many farms are there? What crops do they grow? Prepare a short report for the class on what you find.

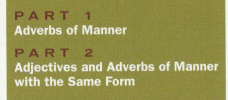

PART 1
Adverbs of Manner

PART 2
Adjectives and Adverbs of Manner
with the Same Form

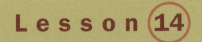
Lesson 14

Psychology: Eating Disorders

■ CONTENT VOCABULARY

Look at the pictures. Do you know the words?

a client

a therapist

therapy

to lose weight

medication

to vomit

patient

to get better
(to recover)

Write the new words in your vocabulary journal.

■ THINK ABOUT IT

Why do some people want to lose weight? How do they lose weight? Do you think people worry about their weight too much? Discuss these questions with your classmates.

■ **GRAMMAR IN CONTENT**

CD1,TR28

A **Read and listen.**

Bulimia

About eight million people in the United States have an eating disorder. One eating disorder is *bulimia nervosa*. Bulimics love to eat, but they want to stay thin. They **secretly** eat a lot of food at one time. Then they **quietly** go to a bathroom and make themselves vomit. This is how they get rid of all the unwanted calories. They also get rid of calories **dangerously** by taking special drugs.

There are other eating disorders. All of these disorders are very destructive, and people with them really need professional help.

a disorder: a sickness or disturbance of the mind or body

to get rid of: to throw away; dispose of

B **Check (✔) *True* or *False*.**

	True	False
1. Bulimics enjoy eating with family and friends.	☐	☐
2. Bulimics don't let much food stay in their bodies.	☐	☐
3. Bulimics get rid of food in two basic ways.	☐	☐
4. Bulimia is safe.	☐	☐

Adverbs of Manner		
Subject	**Verb**	**Adverbs of Manner**
He	ate	quickly. happily. well.

Notes:

- Adverbs of manner describe how we do something.
- To change an adjective into an adverb of manner, add *-ly* (slow—slowly).
- If an adjective ends in a *-y*, change the *-y* to an *-i* and add *-ly* (happy—happily).
- *Well* is the irregular adverb form of *good*.
- When a sentence does not have a direct object, the adverb of manner usually comes after the verb. Example: *He ate quickly.*
- When a sentence has a direct object, put the adverb of manner between the subject and the verb (He **quickly** ate his dinner.) or after the direct object (He ate his dinner **quickly**).
- Never put an adverb of manner between the verb and direct object. NOT *He ate quickly his dinner.*
- *Very* can be added before an adverb of manner. *He ate his dinner **very quickly**.*

C Change the adjectives in parentheses into adverbs of manner. Put each adverb into its sentence. Put the verb into its correct form.

This is Karen. Karen suffers from bulimia. She ___is talking quietly___ **(1)** (talk / quiet) to her friends about the problem. She _____ (sit / **(2)** nervous) and _____ (tell / slow) her friends about the problem. **(3)** Her friends don't know what to do. They _____ (talk / worried) **(4)** to Karen.

Now, her friends _____ (hug / Karen / tight) and **(5)** _____ (tell / her / firm) that she needs to see a doctor. Karen **(6)** _____ (sad / agree). She _____ (brave / **(7)** **(8)** accept) that she's bulimic.

D Read the following conversation between Karen and Dr. Gleason, a physician who specializes in treating eating disorders. (Circle) the adverbs or adjectives to complete the sentences.

Dr. G: I'm very (happy / happily) that you came to see me today, Karen.
(1)

Karen: I am, too, Dr. Gleason. I didn't make this decision (easy / easily), you
(2)
know.

Dr. G: I know, but I think you made a (wise / wisely) decision. Good for you!
(3)

Karen: Doctor, can you treat my eating disorder (quick / quickly)?
(4)

Dr. G: I'm afraid not, Karen. It's a (slow / slowly) process. You will get better
(5)
(slow / slowly).
(6)

E GROUP WORK Work in teams. Each team writes 10 adverbs on separate pieces of paper. Gather all the pieces of paper from each group into one pile. One person from a group picks an adverb. He or she then does something using the adverb. The first team to guess the adverb wins a point.

You're smiling happily.

Right!

PART TWO	Adjectives and Adverbs of Manner with the Same Form

■ GRAMMAR IN CONTENT

A Read and listen.

CD1, TR29

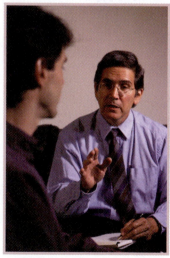

Doctor and Client

Frank: I'm glad that you're talking to me about your problem, Jim.

Jim: I'm working **hard** to face my problem, Frank. You know, you listen better than anybody. Most people don't understand my illness.

Frank: I get it because I was in your shoes many years ago. I know anorexia nervosa **well**.

Jim: My last therapist did things all **wrong**. He didn't even act very friendly. I was afraid to tell him how I really felt.

Frank: You can tell me anything, Jim. Just remember, you won't recover **fast** from your disorder, but you *will* recover if you want to. I promise you that.

anorexia: a prolonged loss of appetite resulting in low body weight

to be in your shoes: to experience what another has experienced

B Check (✔) *True* or *False.*

	True	**False**
1. Frank recently recovered from anorexia nervosa.	☐	☐
2. Jim doesn't want to talk to anybody about his problem.	☐	☐
3. Frank is Jim's new therapist.	☐	☐
4. Jim's previous therapist recommended Frank.	☐	☐
5. Frank knows that most patients need a long time to recover from anorexia.	☐	☐

Adjectives and Adverbs of Manner with the Same Form

	Examples as Adjectives	Examples as Adverbs of Manner
right	She made the **right** decision.	Her therapist is doing her job **right**.
wrong	She didn't make the **wrong** decision.	Her therapist isn't doing her job **wrong**.
fast	You cannot expect a **fast** recovery.	People with eating disorders don't get better **fast**.
hard	Recovery from an eating disorder is **hard**.	She is trying **hard** to get better.
well	I hope you are **well**.	Her therapy sessions went **well**.

C Read each of the following sentences. Decide if the words in *italics* are adjectives or adverbs of manner. Write "adj." for adjective and "adv." for adverb of manner.

1. Understanding eating disorders is *hard* to do. _adj._

2. The therapist is happy with Jim's progress. He thinks he's doing *well*. _____

3. It's *wrong* to think that people with eating disorders are crazy. _____

4. Jim realizes he isn't *well*. He knows he needs therapy. _____

5. Jim changed therapists. It was the *right* thing to do. _____

6. Frank's giving Jim some important lessons about life. He's teaching him *right*. _____

7. Jim's working very *hard* to make a complete recovery. _____

■ COMMUNICATE

D **PAIR WORK** Work with a classmate. Ask and answer the following questions.

What do you do well?   I play the piano well.

1. What do you do well?
2. What do you do fast?
3. What's something you worked hard to have or make?
4. Who do you know that speaks very loudly most of the time?
5. What do you do badly?
6. What's something you did wrong that made you feel sorry?

GRAMMAR AND VOCABULARY Compare the various eating disorders that you learned in this lesson. Use the grammar and vocabulary in this lesson.

PROJECT Prepare a report on eating disorders.

1. Work in small groups.
2. Think about people you know with an eating disorder. This can be bulimia or anorexia, but it can also include overeating (always eating too much), binge eating (like bulimia except victims don't get rid of the food after they eat it), and compulsive eating (using food to fight against stress, depression, etc.). Discuss these people in your group and compare their problems. Describe what they do and how they do it.
3. Write notes about these people.
4. Prepare a presentation to tell the class about the people with eating disorders you discussed.

 INTERNET Go online. Search for clinics that specialize in helping people with eating disorders. Find the following information:

- average length of stay at the clinic
- details about their program
- how they admit somebody
- cost

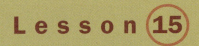

PART 1
As . . . As

PART 2
The Same as, Similar to,
Different from

Lesson 15

Physics:
Standardized
Measures

■ CONTENT VOCABULARY

Look at the pictures. Do you know the words?

Length

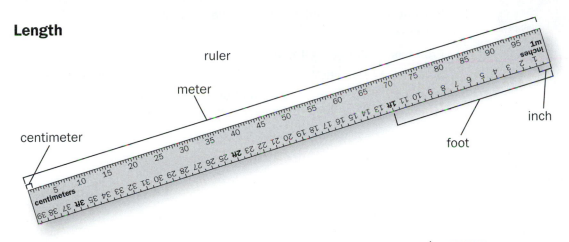

ruler

meter

inch

foot

centimeter

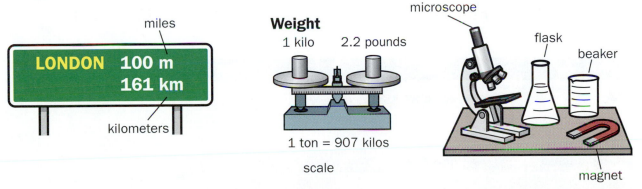

miles

LONDON 100 m
161 km

kilometers

Weight
1 kilo   2.2 pounds

1 ton = 907 kilos

scale

microscope

flask

beaker

magnet

Write the new words in your vocabulary journal.

■ THINK ABOUT IT

How is weight and length measured in different countries? Most countries use one system. The United States uses another. Do you know the differences? Discuss the differences with your class.

■ GRAMMAR IN CONTENT

A **Read and listen.**

CD1,TR30

accurate: exact, correct

In the Lab

Professor:	Now, look carefully at these two blocks. What are the differences between them?
Student:	The big one looks heavier.
Professor:	Actually the big one weighs **as much as** the small one. The small one is made of lead.
	*******
Student A:	Do you know the answer?
Student B:	Yes, sound doesn't travel **as fast as** light.
	*******
Professor:	Can you get that scale?
Student:	This one?
Professor:	No, the other one. That one doesn't work **as well as** the bigger one. It's **not as accurate**.

B **Check (✔)** *True* **or** *False.*

	True	False
1. The lead block is lighter than the big block.	☐	☐
2. Sound travels faster than light does.	☐	☐
3. The professor doesn't like using the smaller scale.	☐	☐

As . . . As		
Be	***as* + adjective + *as***	
A yard **is** almost	**as long as**	a meter.
Simple tense	***as* + adverb + *as***	
Snails **don't move**	**as quickly as**	tigers.
	not as* + adj./adv. + *as	
This scale **is**	not **as accurate as**	the other one.

Notes:

- *As . . . as* means that two things or actions have equal characteristics, equal amounts, or do something equally.
- Use adverbs such as *nearly, almost, about* to indicate that the measure isn't exact.

C Complete each sentence using *as . . . as* and the words in parentheses.

1. An analog clock keeps time (good) _____ as well as _____ a digital clock.

2. A U.S. ton is (not, heavy) _____ a metric ton.

3. 100° Celsius is (hot) _____ 212° Fahrenheit.

4. Going at the same speed, you can't run a mile (quick)

   _____ you can run a kilometer.

5. Two pounds is (almost much) _____ one kilo.

6. Lab mice are not (free) _____ field mice.

D Look at the pictures. Write two sentences about each picture using the words in parentheses. Use *as . . . as* for the first sentence and *not as . . . as* for the second.

A   B

1. (nearly, big) __ Magnet A is nearly as big as Magnet B. __

2. (powerful) _____

A   B

3. (almost, much liquid) _____

4. (clean) _____

A   B

5. (old) _____

6. (useful) _____

■ **C O M M U N I C A T E**

E **PAIR WORK** Compare yourself to a classmate. Use the words and phrases in the box. Use (*not*) *as . . . as* to make comparisons.

age	height	distance from home to school	ease at learning grammar

I'm 27. How old are you?

I'm 45. You're not as old as I am.

■ GRAMMAR IN CONTENT

A Read and listen to the following passage.

CD1,TR31

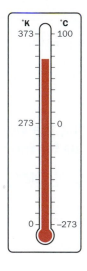

From Hands to Standard Units

Thousands of years ago people used their hands and feet to measure length. But one person's hand is usually **not the same as** another person's hand. The length of one person's foot is **different from** another person's foot. This kind of system isn't very precise. Science requires exact measurement.

Today, physicists use the International System of Units (SI) for measuring things. For example, the standard unit of length is the *meter*. The standard unit of light is the *candela*. Many of these standard units are **similar to** ones you know, such as the *meter*, *minute*, and *kilogram*. Some standard units are **different**. For example, the standard unit for temperature is Kelvin, not Celsius or Fahrenheit. 300° Kelvin is **the same as** 81°F or 27°C.

precise: exact

B Check (✔) *True* or *False*.

	True	False
1. A long time ago, people used the body to measure length.	☐	☐
2. Without standardization, measuring things is confusing.	☐	☐
3. Today everybody uses the same system for weights and measures.	☐	☐
4. Standardized weights and measures are important for science.	☐	☐

The Same as, Similar to, and *Different from*		
Noun Phrase	**Comparative Phrase**	**Noun Phrase**
One meter is	**the same** (length) **as** **similar to** **different from**	3,281 feet. three feet. one foot.

Note:
• We can use *the same, similar,* and *different* without a preposition + noun or noun phrase if the other person understands what we're talking about. *Their money is **different**, but their way of measuring temperature is **the same**.*

C Look at the following pictures. Complete each sentence with *the same as,* *similar to,* or *different from.*

1 year = 365 days

1 year = 687 Earth days

1. An African elephant is

   similar to

   an Asian elephant.

2. Earth's orbit is

   _____

   Mars's orbit.

Mt. Shasta   Mt. Rainier

14,162 feet   14,410 feet

A   B

3. The height of Mt. Shasta is

   _____

   Mt. Rainier's.

4. Magnet A is

   _____

   Magnet B.

D Read each of the following descriptions. Write an observation about the information. Use *the same,* *similar to,* and *different from.*

1. The boiling point for water in Fahrenheit is 212°. In Celsius it is 100°.

   The boiling point for water in Fahrenheit is different from the boiling point in Celsius.

2. The length of an ancient Egyptian cubit was about 45 cm. The length of a Roman cubit was about 120 cm.

   _____.

3. Ball A is moving at a speed of 20 kph. Ball C is moving at 21 kph.

   _____.

4. Emma's height is 1.74 m. Sam's height is also 1.74 m.

   _____.

5. A humpback whale travels 11,000 miles every year. Gray whales travel 11,500 miles.

   _____.

6. The weight of Block A is 10 kg. The weight of Block B is 1 kg.

   _____.

E WRITE Write a short paragraph describing people and things in your life. Use *the same as, similar to,* and *different from* in your sentences.

My House vs. My Uncle's House

The size of our house is similar to my uncle's house. They both have the same number of bedrooms and bathrooms. Our driveways are the same length. The size of our kitchens is different. His kitchen is larger than ours.

Connection | Putting It Together

GRAMMAR AND VOCABULARY Work with a classmate. Talk about the following topics. Use the grammar and vocabulary from the lesson.

1. the weather today compared to last week
2. your house compared to your partner's
3. your work or studies compared to your partner's
4. your commute to class compared to your partner's

 INTERNET PROJECT Write a report on two countries.

1. Work in small groups.
2. Choose two countries you know well. Take notes about what's similar or different about these countries. Here are suggestions for topics to compare, but you can use other or additional topics, too:

   - size of the countries
   - number of large cities
   - legal speed on highways
   - population
   - age of capital city
   - climate

3. Use the Internet to find out the information you need. Prepare a report comparing your two countries. Present the report to your class.

A Complete the conversation between two friends. In some blanks, you should put nothing. Use the words in parentheses to compare things.

Harry: I'm sorry to disagree with you, but _____(1) cats are (smart) _____(2) _____(3) dogs.

Carla: What? No way! _____(4) cat that my brother has isn't _____(5) smart _____(6) my dog.

Harry: Listen, _____(7) cat can control its owner, especially with _____(8) food. _____(9) dog can eat the _____(10) thing every day, but _____(11) cats don't like that. _____(12) cat owner gives his cat _____(13) kinds of _____(14) food. So which pet is (smart) _____(15)?

Carla: _____(16) dogs are (good) _____(17) pets _____(18) cats because they protect _____(19) houses and _____(20) people. For protection, no pet is (bad) _____(21) _____(22) cat! In fact, _____(23) dog in _____(24) house next to mine saved her owner's life!

Harry: You can say anything you want, but the numbers show which pet is _____(25) popular. There are (few) _____(26) dogs in this country _____(27) cats. The government says so. _____(28) cat is (easy) _____(29) to take care of, (cute) _____(30), and (interesting) _____(31) _____(32) dog!

Harry: You know what? Let's stop arguing. We're never going to agree.

B Complete this conversation between a nutritionist and her client. Use the words in parentheses in their correct form. Use quantifiers, too.

Nutritionist: You're still overweight, Margaret. You're eating _____(1) calories each day. I know you're working (hard) _____(2) to lose weight, but there's a problem.

Margaret: But I try to eat (careful) _____ . I don't eat
(3)
_____ fat and I don't eat (fast) _____ .
(4)   (5)
I enjoy every bite of food and eat (slow) _____ . You
(6)
mean I'm not doing this (right) _____ ?
(7)

Nutritionist: No, you're doing that (correct) _____ . Do you eat
(8)
breakfast every day?

Margaret: Well, no, I don't. I only have lunch and dinner.

Nutritionist: That's not good. You're eating _____ meals per
(9)
day. You should have breakfast. Your body will work (efficient)
_____ if you have breakfast. It will burn
(10)
_____ calories.
(11)

Margaret: Really? I didn't know that. I thought it would be (good)
_____ to eat (little) _____ food than
(12)   (13)
_____ .
(14)

Nutritionist: _____ food, yes, but _____ meals, no.
(15)   (16)
Do you eat potatoes, rice, and pasta?

Margaret: Yes, but just _____ . I know they have
(17)
_____ calories.
(18)

LEARNER LOG Check (✔) *Yes* or *I Need More Practice.*

Lesson	I Can Use . . .	Yes	I Need More Practice
11	The Ø Article, *A/An,* and *The*		
12	Quantifiers and *Too Many/Too Few, Too Much/Too Little*		
13	Regular and Irregular Comparative Adjectives		
14	Adverbs of Manner Ending in *-ly* and Adjectives and Adverbs of Manner with the Same Form		
15	*As . . . As, The Same as, Similar to,* and *Different from*		

PART 1
The Simple Past Tense:
Statements with Regular Verbs

PART 2
The Simple Past Tense: *Yes/No*
Questions and Short Answers

L e s s o n (16)

U.S. History: Immigration

■ CONTENT VOCABULARY

Look at the pictures. Do you know the words?

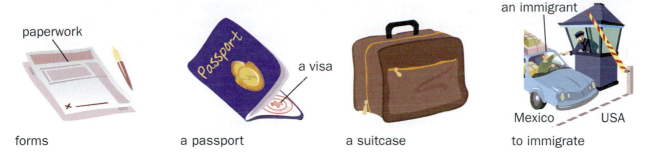

paperwork

forms

a passport

a visa

a suitcase

an immigrant

Mexico   USA

to immigrate

Write the new words in your vocabulary journal.

■ THINK ABOUT IT

What causes people to immigrate to other countries? Discuss this with your classmates.

■ **GRAMMAR IN CONTENT**

CD2,TR1

A **Read and listen.**

The Irish Potato Famine

The United States is a nation of immigrants. One of the biggest groups of immigrants **arrived** from Ireland in the 1850s. Why did they come to the United States? They **escaped** the Potato Famine.

The Irish Potato Famine **happened** between 1845 and 1849. A disease **destroyed** the potatoes in Ireland. Potatoes were the main food for people in Ireland. People **didn't have** enough food to eat. Nearly one million people **died** in the famine. Many Irish **didn't want** to live in Ireland anymore. Nearly two million people **immigrated** to the United States. They **traveled** by ship and **landed** in cities such as Boston, New York, and Philadelphia. Most of the Irish families **stayed** in these cities. The 1850 census in Boston **showed** that over 25% of the people were Irish immigrants.

The famine **changed** Ireland and the United States forever.

to escape: to get away from someone or something

a census: a count of the people in the country by the government

B **Check (✔) *True* or *False*.**

	True	False
1. Many Irish came to the United States in the 1800s.	☐	☐
2. The famine lasted for four years.	☐	☐
3. A disease attacked the potatoes.	☐	☐
4. All Irish immigrants stayed in Boston.	☐	☐

The Simple Past Tense Affirmative Statements		
Subject	Base Form of Verb + -d/-ed	
I You He She It We They	arrived	yesterday. in 1984. a year ago.

The Simple Past Tense Negative Statements		
Subject	did + not	Base Form of Verb
I You He She It We They	did not (OR) didn't	arrive

(Negative statements time expressions: last week. this morning. a month ago.)

Notes:

- Use the simple past tense when an action is finished. Example: *Many animals **walked** from Siberia to Alaska millions of years ago.*
- Also use the simple past tense when a condition is finished. Example: *She **wanted** a better life.*
- To make the negative, use *did not (**didn't**) + verb.* Example: *She **did not (didn't) want** the same life.*
- Regular verbs in the simple past end with *-d, -ed,* or *-ied.* Examples: *arrived, worked, studied.*
- Regular verbs in the simple past have three different sounds at the end: */d/, /t/,* and */id/.* Examples: *arrived (/d/), worked (/t/), wanted (/id/).*

C Listen to the past tense pronunciation of these verbs. You will hear each verb twice. On the blank line after each verb, write */d/, /t/,* or */id/* for the final sound you hear. Number 1 is an example.

CD2,TR2

1. climbed   /d/   6. lived _____ 11. crossed _____

2. travel _____ 7. started _____ 12. wanted _____

3. forced _____ 8. looked _____ 13. joined _____

4. captured _____ 9. stayed _____ 14. matched _____

5. decided _____ 10. received _____ 15. immigrated _____

D Read the conversation. Fill in the blanks with the verbs in parentheses. Use present or past forms. Use affirmative and negative forms.

Nadia: Hi. My name's Nadia. I _____ (see) you in here last week.
(1)

_____ (you / live) in the neighborhood?
(2)

Bossi: Yes. We _____ (live) around the corner on Mulberry
(3)

Street. We _____ (move) here from Nigeria three weeks
(4)

ago. My name's Bossi.

Nadia: Nigeria? That's interesting. I _____ (immigrate) here
(5)

with my family almost a year ago. We're from Slovakia.

Bossi: I _____ (have) a hard time in this new country.
(6)

Nadia: I _____ (understand). Life _____ (be) easy
(7)   (8)

for us when we _____ (arrive). But it's much better now.
(9)

_____ (you / be) here with your husband?
(10)

Bossi: No, with my sister and brother-in-law. My husband _____
(11)
(travel) with us. He's still in Nigeria. He _____ (need) a
(12)
passport.

Nadia: We _____ (need) all kinds of paperwork to come here.
(13)
I'm very happy that we _____ (finish) all the paperwork
(14)
before our trip.

Bossi: That was good. Well, my laundry's done. I have to get home. Nice
meeting you, Nadia.

Nadia: Nice meeting you, too. I hope I see you again, Bossi. 'Bye.

E Rewrite the following sentences. Use the pronoun in parentheses, and negative
simple past statements.

1. She wanted to immigrate. (they) _____ They didn't want to immigrate. _____

2. He needed a passport. (she) _____

3. We traveled for a long time. (they) _____

4. I expected to have an easy life. (you) _____

5. She immigrated to Spain. (he) _____

6. You changed your plans. (we) _____

F Look at the pictures of Sasha. Write simple sentences that contrast his old life
in Belarus with his new one in the United States. Use the verbs in parentheses to
help you.

Belarus   U.S.A.

1. (live) _____ Sasha lived on a farm in Belarus. _____

2. (live) _____ Now Sasha lives in an apartment building. _____

3. (work) _____

4. (drive) _____

5. (always need) _____

6. (have) _____

7. (watch) _____

8. (play) _____

Minsk

Sasha's Farm

Belarus

9. (travel) _____

10. (doesn't travel) _____

■ C O M M U N I C A T E

G WRITE How is your life now different from the past? Write a paragraph describing the changes. Use the simple past tense.

■ **GRAMMAR IN CONTENT**

A Read and listen to this conversation between two college students.

CD2,TR3

Ellis Island

Jack: What's that book, Renée?

Renée: It's a history of Ellis Island. **Did** you **learn** about it in high school?

Jack: Yes, **I did.**

Renée: **Did** your family **arrive** in America at Ellis Island?

Jack: Yes, **they did.** Almost all my friends' families started life in America at Ellis Island. It was the most important place to greet and process immigrants on the east coast of the U.S. Then, the government closed it because the buildings were too old.

Renée: **Did** they **close** it recently?

Jack: No, they didn't. They closed it about 60 years ago. **Did** your history instructor **recommend** that book?

Renée: Yes, **she did.** My family arrived in the U.S. at Ellis Island, too.

to greet: to say hello   **to process:** to apply a procedure to someone or something

a coast: land near the ocean   **to recommend:** to tell others about something or someone you like

B Check (✔) *True* or *False*.

	True	False
1. Jack's family arrived at Ellis Island.	☐	☐
2. Renée's family arrived in Canada.	☐	☐
3. Ellis Island operates now.	☐	☐
4. Renée is reading the book for college.	☐	☐

The Simple Past Tense: *Yes/No* Questions				
The Simple Past Tense				**Short Answers**
Did	**Subject**	**Base Form of Verb**		
Did	I			Yes, I **did.** / No, I **didn't.**
	you			Yes, you **did.** / No, you **didn't.**
	he		last week?	Yes, he **did.** / No, he **didn't.**
	she	arrive	this morning?	Yes, she **did.** / No, she **didn't.**
	it		a month ago?	Yes, it **did.** / No, it **didn't.**
	we			Yes, we **did.** / No, we **didn't.**
	they			Yes, they **did.** / No, they **didn't.**

C Rewrite the following sentences in the simple past tense to make them *Yes/No* questions. Then complete the short answers.

1. Renée's family arrived in America at Ellis Island.

   Did Renée's family arrive in America at Ellis Island? Yes, _they did._

2. They wanted to leave their country for political reasons.

   _____ No, _____

3. Immigrants traveled to America by plane in those days.

   _____ No, _____

4. Renée's father explained the family history to her.

   _____ Yes, _____

5. Her family found a better life in America than in the "old country."

   _____ Yes, _____

6. A very dramatic period of immigration happened between 1880 and 1930.

   _____ Yes, _____

7. Renée emigrated from the old country.

   _____ No, _____

■ COMMUNICATE

D **PAIR WORK** Look again at the pictures in exercise F in Part One. Ask and answer questions about Sasha's life today and in the past.

Did Sasha live on a farm in Belarus?

Yes, he did.

E PAIR WORK Work with a classmate. Think about a trip you took. It could be a vacation or when you immigrated to a different country. Ask questions in the simple past tense using the words below.

1. need / tickets?
2. need / visa?
3. pack / suitcase?
4. arrive / plane or boat?
5. travel / alone?

 Did you need tickets?

 No, I didn't.

Connection | Putting It Together

GRAMMAR AND VOCABULARY Share your family history with three or four classmates. Talk about relatives who immigrated to your country or emigrated from your country. Compare stories. Use the grammar and vocabulary in this lesson.

 INTERNET PROJECT Prepare a report on immigrants.

1. Work with a classmate. Choose an ethnic group in the United States. For example, you might choose Irish, Haitian, Italian, German, or Chinese.
2. Find information about that group on the Internet.
3. Fill in the blanks with the main information.

Name of ethnic group:

_____

Start of their immigration to the United States:

_____

Reason(s) for their emigration:

_____

Location(s) in the United States where this group lives in large numbers:

_____

Famous Americans from this group:

_____

4. Write a short paragraph in your notebook using this information. With your classmate, present the information to the class.

PART 1
The Simple Past Tense:
Irregular Verbs

PART 2
The Simple Past Tense:
Information Questions

PART 3
Before and *After* in the Simple
Past Tense

Lesson 17

Medicine: History of Medicine

■ CONTENT VOCABULARY

Look at the pictures. Do you know the words?

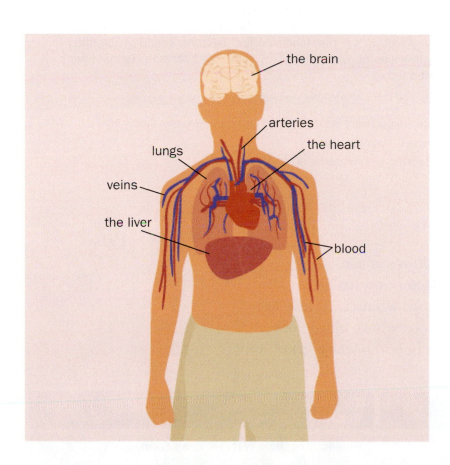

the brain

arteries

the heart

lungs

veins

the liver

blood

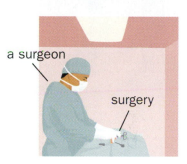

a surgeon

surgery

an operation

herbs

traditional medicine

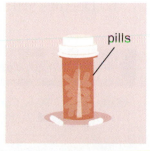

pills

modern medicine

Write the new words in your vocabulary journal.

■ THINK ABOUT IT

How is medicine different now than it was long ago? Discuss this question with the class.

■ GRAMMAR IN CONTENT

CD2,TR4

A **Read and listen.**

The Beginnings of Medicine: Part I

The field of modern medicine **began** in Egypt almost five thousand years ago. Imhotep was the ancient Egyptian "father" of medicine. He lived from 2635 to 2595 BCE. Imhotep **taught** Egyptian doctors about basic medicine during that time.

Imhotep, along with other Egyptians, **made** some important medical discoveries. They **saw** that blood traveled through arteries, veins, and the heart. They **fought** diseases with medicines from plants and animals. They **understood** a lot about the heart and brain, but they **thought** that intelligence was in the heart, not the brain.

Many doctors say that medicine first **became** a field of scientific study in ancient Egypt. This is why some medical schools still honor Imhotep today.

BCE: "Before the Common Era." The Common Era is now more than 2,000 years old.

a discovery: to find something new

to honor: to praise, give recognition to

B **Check (✔)** *True* **or** *False.*

	True	False
1. Imhotep lived over 5,000 years ago.	☐	☐
2. Imhotep was a great doctor and teacher.	☐	☐
3. The Egyptians understood what the brain does.	☐	☐
4. The Egyptians understood where blood goes.	☐	☐
5. Doctors still think that Imhotep was a great man.	☐	☐

The Simple Past Tense Affirmative Statements		The Simple Past Tense Negative Statements		
Subject	Past Form of Verb	Subject	*Did + Not*	Base Form of Verb
I		I		
You		You		
He		He	**did not**	
She	**made** a discovery.	She	**(OR)**	**make** a discovery.
It		It	**didn't**	
We		We		
They		They		

Notes:

- Irregular verbs do not have the *-ed* ending in the past tense. Examples:

be – was	do – did	give – gave	read – read
begin – began	drink – drank	go – went	take – took
become – became	eat – ate	have – had	teach – taught
break – broke	feel – felt	keep – kept	think – thought
come – came	find – found	know – knew	write – wrote
cut – cut	fight – fought	leave – left	

- See the appendix on page 241 for more irregular verbs and their simple past forms.

C Fill in the blanks using the verbs in the box below. Put them in the simple past tense. Use the affirmative or negative as necessary.

read	find	~~begin~~	know	have	keep	write

The field of medicine ___*began*___ (1) in Egypt nearly 5,000 years ago. Before then, people _____ (2) much about medicine. The ancient Egyptians _____ (3) a basic understanding of how our bodies work.

Imhotep and other Egyptian doctors _____ (4) records of their work. These doctors _____ (5) about their medical discoveries on papyrus, the first paper. Many years later, people _____ (6) the papyrus and _____ (7) about the medical discoveries.

D Write short answers and then write complete answers to the following questions. Use the simple past tense.

1. **Q:** Did Imhotep come from Egypt?

   A: (Yes) _____ Yes, he did. Imhotep came from Egypt. _____

2. **Q:** Did Imhotep give the world important medical information?

   A: (Yes) _____

3. **Q:** Did ancient Egyptians have many doctors?

   A: (No) _____

4. **Q:** Did Imhotep teach other Egyptians about medicine?

    A: (Yes) _____

5. **Q:** Did some Egyptian physicians leave records of their work?

    A: (Yes) _____

6. **Q:** Did the Egyptians think that the brain was the center of intelligence?

    A: (No) _____

7. **Q:** Did Imohotep go to patients' houses?

    A: (Yes) _____

8. **Q:** Did ancient Egyptian doctors fight diseases that we still have today?

    A: (Yes) _____

■ **C O M M U N I C A T E**

E PAIR WORK Think about a time when you had an accident or illness. Ask your classmate *Yes/No* questions in the simple past tense. Use the ideas in the box below.

feel very sick	break a bone	cut yourself seriously by accident
go to the hospital	have an operation	take prescription drugs

Did you feel very sick? — Yes, I did. I was very sick.

F GROUP WORK Work in groups of three. Write down ten irregular verbs in the past tense on different pieces of paper *(had, flew, etc.)*. Write down ten time words or phrases *(yesterday, last year, etc.)*. Put the pieces of paper face down on the table. Take turns turning over one verb and one time phrase. Make true sentences using the words.

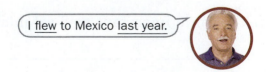

I flew to Mexico last year.

■ GRAMMAR IN CONTENT

CD2,TR5

A Read and listen to the following conversation.

a caduceus

Hippocrates

> **The Beginnings of Medicine: Part II**
>
> Prof: Does anyone have any questions?
>
> Emily: Yes. **Why did** they **put** snakes on the caduceus?
>
> Prof: People thought that snakes never got sick. Pictures of snakes were used as a protection against disease.
>
> Jana: **Who created** the caduceus as a symbol of medicine?
>
> Prof: The ancient Greeks in the time of Hippocrates.
>
> Henri: I know that Hippocrates is the father of medicine, but **where did** he **work?**
>
> Prof: On the island of Kos.
>
> Henri: In Greece, right? **When did** Hippocrates **live?**
>
> Prof: From 460 to 377 BCE, a long time after Imhotep.
>
> Emily: **What did** Hippocrates **do** that made him famous?
>
> Prof: He built the first school of medicine. It was on Kos. He also said for the first time that being sick was not a punishment from angry gods. All his students had to take an oath to be the best doctors they could be. We still use it today. We call it the Hippocratic Oath.

a symbol: a sign, mark, or picture that represents something else

a punishment: what happens when you do something wrong

an oath: a promise to do something

B Check (✔) *True* or *False.*

	True	False
1. Snakes on the caduceus are symbols of protection.	☐	☐
2. Imhotep created the caduceus.	☐	☐
3. Hippocrates worked in Athens.	☐	☐
4. Hippocrates built the first school of medicine in Athens.	☐	☐

Information Questions in the Simple Past Tense			
Wh- Word *How* Phrase	*Did*	Subject	Verb
When Where How long ago	did	Hippocrates	teach medicine?

Information Questions in the Simple Past Tense

Who or What as Subject	Past Simple Verb	Object	Additions
Who	made	medicines	from plants in ancient Greece?
What	caused	malaria	in people?

Notes:

- When *who* and *what* are the subjects of a question in the past, don't use the auxiliary *did*. (See the examples in the chart.)
- When *who* and *what* are the objects of a question in the past, use the auxiliary *did*. Examples: **Who(m) did you** *think was the father of medicine?* ("You" is the subject.) **What did Hippocrates** *believe was the cause of disease?* ("Hippocrates" is the subject.)

C **Put the words in the correct order to make information questions.**

1. **Q:** the first school of medicine – Hippocrates – open – did – where?

   _____ *Where did Hippocrates open the first school of medicine?* _____

   A: He opened it on the island of Kos.

2. **Q:** live – Hippocrates – did – how long ago?

   _____

   A: He lived almost 2,400 years ago.

3. **Q:** use – what – as the symbol of the medical profession – did – the Greeks?

   _____

   A: They used the caduceus.

4. **Q:** and work – when – Hippocrates – live – did?

   _____

   A: He lived and worked in the fifth and fourth centuries BCE.

5. **Q:** snakes – the Greeks – why – on the caduceus – did – put?

   _____

   A: Because they were a symbol of protection from sickness.

D Look at the dialogues below. The underlined part is the answer. Write a question for the answer.

1. **Q:** *Who(m) did Hippocrates teach?*

   A: Hippocrates taught <u>medical students.</u>

2. **Q:** _____

   A: Hippocrates wrote a <u>famous oath.</u>

3. **Q:** _____

   A: Hippocrates' patients were <u>the people on the island of Kos.</u>

4. **Q:** _____

   A: Hippocrates became famous <u>in the fifth century BCE.</u>

5. **Q:** _____

   A: Hippocrates traveled to Italy <u>three times</u> to teach medical students there.

6. **Q:** _____

   A: <u>Doctors in later centuries</u> called Hippocrates "the father of medicine."

7. **Q:** _____

   A: Hippocrates opened the first school of medicine on Kos <u>because that is where he lived.</u>

■ C O M M U N I C A T E

E **PAIR WORK** Look back at exercise E in Part One. Ask a classmate follow-up questions about his/her sickness.

F **WRITE** Write about what you found out in exercise E.

> Claudio's brother had appendicitis. That happened ten years ago. He became sick in Bogotá, Colombia, his hometown. He went to the hospital and had an appendectomy. He was in the hospital for three days. The surgeon took out his appendix.

GRAMMAR IN CONTENT

A Read and listen.

CD2,TR6

Shen Nong the Herbalist

Before the Egyptians and the Greeks learned about the human body, the ancient Chinese understood many things about it.

Around 2800 BCE, the physician Shen Nong discovered the power of herbs. They could help people fight diseases. Shen Nong made a kind of tea using different herbs. **Before** he made the tea, he chose special herbs for it. **After** he made the tea, he gave it to his patients. He saw that **after** they drank the tea, the patients got better. **After** his patients got better, he wrote down the results. He wrote a book full of his observations.

This was the beginning of traditional Chinese medicine. **After** almost 5,000 years, Chinese doctors still use Shen Nong's book to treat their patients.

to write down: to write on paper

a result: an effect; a consequence of an action

to treat: to give medical attention to

B Check (✔) True or False.

	True	False
1. Chinese medicine is older than Egyptian medicine.	☐	☐
2. Shen Nong lived around the same time as Imhotep.	☐	☐
3. Shen Nong lived and worked in the second millennium BCE.	☐	☐
4. Shen Nong's patients ate different kinds of herbs.	☐	☐

The Simple Past Tense: *Before, After*	
Before, After	**Statement in the Simple Past**
Before I **went** to the doctor, **After** I **left** the doctor's office,	I **made** an appointment. I **got** some medicine from the pharmacy.

Notes:

• In a sentence with *before* or *after* there are two clauses (parts).

• When the clause with *before* or *after* comes first, use a comma (,) to separate the two clauses.

C Complete each sentence with *before* or *after*.

1. __Before__ Hippocrates was born, Shen Nong studied medicine.

2. _____ Imhotep learned about medicine, he became a medical teacher.

3. _____ Hippocrates practiced medicine, there were no medical schools in Greece.

4. Shen Nong wrote about herbal medicine _____ he made his observations.

5. _____ Imhotep became a doctor, he traveled all over Egypt.

6. A few centuries passed _____ the Egyptians made Imhotep the god of medicine.

D Look at the pictures. Write a sentence about what happened using the words in parentheses.

1. (after / run / not feel well)

After he ran, he didn't feel well.

2. (before / fall / drank a glass of water)

_____

_____

3. (after / find / call for help)

_____

_____

4. (after / take / have an operation)

_____

_____

5. (before / leave / thank the doctor)

_____

_____

E Complete the sentences with information about yourself.

1. Before I had breakfast today, _____.

2. Before I came to class today, _____.

3. After I finished kindergarten, _____.

4. Before my parents had me, _____.

5. After I _____.

6. Before I _____.

■ COMMUNICATE

F **WRITE** Write a paragraph comparing traditional medicine and modern medicine. What are their strengths and weaknesses?

Connection — Putting It Together

GRAMMAR AND VOCABULARY Talk to three or four classmates about a past illness you, a member of your family, or a friend had. Share your story with the others. Use the grammar and vocabulary in this lesson.

PROJECT Role-play a conversation between Imhotep and Hippocrates.

1. Work in pairs. Imagine you are Imhotep and Hippocrates talking about medicine. Decide who will play each role.
2. Write a dialogue that they might have had. Use examples of the simple past tense.
3. Practice the conversation.
4. Present your conversation to the whole class.

 INTERNET Go online. Search for a famous person in medical history from your country or another country. Find out some interesting facts about the person and write down the information. Write about the facts in a short paragraph and present your findings to the class.

PART 1
The Past Progressive: Statements

PART 2
The Past Progressive: Questions

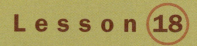

Lesson 18

Geology: Early Mammals

■ CONTENT VOCABULARY

Look at the pictures. Do you know the words?

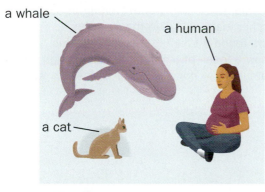

a whale

a human

a cat

mammals

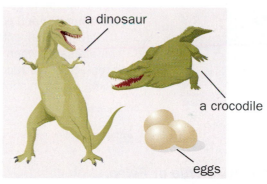

a dinosaur

a crocodile

eggs

reptiles

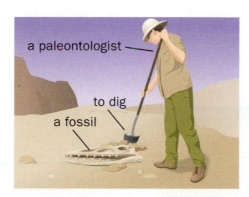

a paleontologist

to dig

a fossil

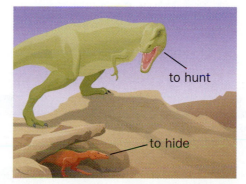

to hunt

to hide

Write the new words in your vocabulary journal.

■ THINK ABOUT IT

What do you know about dinosaurs? Where did dinosaurs live? Did dinosaurs come from mammals? Did mammals come from dinosaurs? Discuss these questions with your classmates.

■ GRAMMAR IN CONTENT

CD2, TR7

A Read and listen.

an eomaia

a repenomamus

Mammals and Dinosaurs

Many people think that mammals only appeared after the dinosaurs became extinct. But, in fact, dinosaurs and mammals **were living** together on Earth at the same time. Mammals lived with their dinosaur neighbors for over 130 million years.

But what **were** these mammals **doing** during this time? The eomaia, a mammal the size of a mouse, **was hiding** from the meat-eating dinosaurs and **eating** insects and fruits. Eomaias **were living** in trees because life on the ground was too dangerous. Repenomamuses, mammals as large as a medium-size dog, **weren't hiding** at all. They **were hunting** and **eating** other mammals, like the eomaias.

Recently, paleontologists found a fossil of a repenomamus. They were amazed when they saw a fossil of a small dinosaur inside the stomach of the repenomamus. They now know that dinosaurs **weren't doing** all the hunting.

extinct: no longer in existence

B Check (✔) *True* or *False*.

	True	False
1. The eomaia was the size of a dog.	☐	☐
2. The eomaia didn't fight dinosaurs because it was too small.	☐	☐
3. The repenomamus was a meat eater.	☐	☐

The Past Progressive: Statements

Subject	*Be* in the Past	Verb + *-ing*	
I He She	was was not		
You We They	were were not	looking	for fossils last week.

Notes:

• Use the past progressive to talk about an action already happening at a specific time in the past.

• Use the contraction (*wasn't/weren't*) in speech and informal writing.

C **Circle** the correct verb in each of the following sentences.

1. Mammals (was living / (were living)) on Earth with the dinosaurs.
2. Mammals (was sharing / were sharing) Earth with dinosaurs.
3. The eomaia (was surviving / were surviving) by running away from dinosaurs.
4. The fossils (was lying / were lying) in the ground for millions of years.
5. Chinese scientists (was looking for / were looking for) fossils at the time of the eomaia's discovery.

D Use the verbs in parentheses to complete the sentences. Use the past progressive.

Clyde: Where were you yesterday afternoon? I ___was looking___ (look)
(1)

everywhere for you.

Harry: I _____ (help) Rhoda all afternoon. We
(2)

_____ (digging) for fossils near the lake. It took a long
(3)

time. We _____ (not / watch) the time. We didn't finish
(4)

until 10 o'clock. Why were you looking for me?

Clyde: I _____ (listening) to the news around noon. They
(5)

discovered more eomaia fossils in China!

Harry: Really?

Clyde: Yes. Palentologists _____ (look) for dinosaur fossils, but
(6)

they found eomaia fossils instead.

E Complete the dialogues with negative past progressive statements.

1. **A:** I saw you studying in the library yesterday.

   B: It wasn't me. I ___wasn't studying___ in the library yesterday.

2. **A:** Was the instructor talking about dinosaurs?

   B: No, she _____.

3. **A:** Were they talking to her?

   B: No, _____.

4. **A:** At midnight, I was sleeping.

   B: Lucky you. I _____ my homework.

F Look at the picture below. Write a paragraph about what was and wasn't happening yesterday. Use the past progressive and the verbs in the box.

dig   walk   hide   eat   drive   read   drink   talk

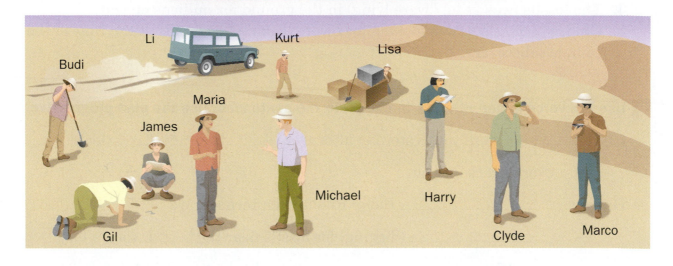

_____

_____

_____

_____

_____

■ **COMMUNICATE**

G **PAIR WORK** Tell a classmate what you, your family, or your friends were or were not doing at 8 o'clock last night.

At 8:00 I was watching a documentary about dinosaurs. And you?

I wasn't watching TV. I was driving to my sister's house.

H **WRITE** Write down what you found out about your classmate in exercise G.

> At 8 o'clock last night, Magda wasn't watching TV at home.
> She was driving to her sister's house. Her sister was expecting her.

■ GRAMMAR IN CONTENT

A **Read and listen.**

CD2,TR8

Egg Layers, Marsupials, and Placentals

Kurt: **Were** the mammals in the Mesozoic Era all **reproducing** the same way, Professor?

Prof: **No, they weren't,** Kurt.

Kurt: **What were** they **doing** that was different?

Prof: About 160 million years ago, three groups of mammals evolved. One group laid eggs. A second group we call marsupials had a pouch for the baby to develop in, like a kangaroo. A third group had a placenta so the baby could develop inside the mother. We call this third group placentals. Most mammals today are placentals.

Kurt: **Why were** they **evolving** so differently?

Prof: We really don't know, Kurt.

Kurt: **Where was** all of this **happening?**

Prof: We found fossils in China, so we know that they **were developing** there. But we don't know why there are different kinds of mammals.

to evolve: to develop, change over time

B **Check (✔) *True, False,* or *Don't know.***

	True	False	Don't know
1. There were two kinds of mammals during the Mesozoic Era.	☐	☐	☐
2. The repenomamus was a placental.	☐	☐	☐
3. Marsupial babies develop in their mother's pouch.	☐	☐	☐
4. Dinosaurs were also placentals.	☐	☐	☐
5. The eomaia was a placental.	☐	☐	☐

The Past Progressive: *Yes/No* Questions

Yes/No Question			Short Answer
Was/Were	**Subject**	**Verb + *-ing***	**Affirmative**
Was	I he she		Yes, you were. No, you were not (weren't).
		learning about fossils?	
Were	you we they		Yes, we were. No, we were not (weren't).

The Past Progressive: Information Questions			
Wh- Words **How Phrases**	**Be**	**Subject**	**Verb + -ing**
What Who(m)	was	I he she it	**looking** for?
Where Why How long	were	you we they	**studying** paleontology?

C **Look at the picture of Dr. Stan Chung. Complete the questions and answers about what he was doing.**

1. **Q:** (Dr. Chung / study / paleontology / in 1991?)

   Was Dr. Chung studying paleontology in 1991?

   A: (yes) _Yes, he was._

2. **Q:** (he / plan / to be a doctor?)

   _____

   A: (no) _____

3. **Q:** (he / plan / to become a paleontologist?)

   _____

   A: (yes) _____

4. **Q:** (he / work / in China / in 1994?)

   _____

   A: (yes) _____

5. **Q:** (why / he / work / in China?)

   _____

   A: (look for fossils) _____

D **Write questions for the answers. Use the past progressive.**

Interviewer: (What?) _____What were you looking for?_____

Dr. Chung: We were looking for fossils.

Interviewer: (Where?) _____

Dr. Chung: Mostly in northeastern China.

Interviewer: (What?) _____

Dr. Chung: We were expecting to find dinosaur fossils.

Interviewer: (Where?) _____

Dr. Chung: The fossils were lying on the ground.

Interviewer: (Why?) _____

Dr. Chung: We're not sure why they were lying on the ground. Perhaps the wind blew the soil away and uncovered them.

■ **C O M M U N I C A T E**

E **PAIR WORK** **Look at Dr. Chung's diary. Work with a classmate. Ask and answer questions about his day using the past progressive.**

What was he doing at 8:00? — He was eating breakfast.

8:00	Breakfast
9:00	Office hours
10:00	Interview w/ *The Big Dig Weekly* (about my new book)
11:00	
12:00	Faculty meeting – Conference Room 1
1:00	Lunch
2:00	Paleontology lecture (Rm. 320D)

F **GROUP WORK** Ask and answer information questions using the prompts below. Ask follow-up questions.

1. before class
2. in 2004
3. at lunchtime yesterday
4. last summer
5. on your last birthday

What were you doing before class?

I was working.

Where were you working?

Connection | Putting It Together

GRAMMAR AND VOCABULARY Work with a classmate. Look at the picture below. Ask and answer questions about what was happening.

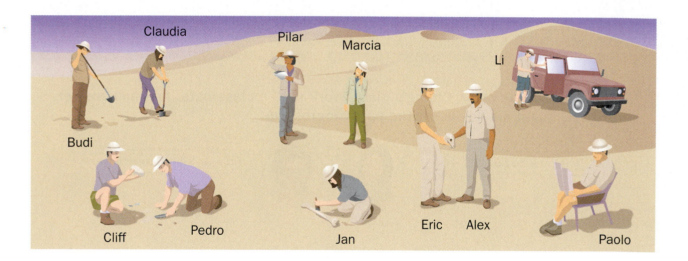

 INTERNET PROJECT Work with one or two classmates. Search on the Internet for information on mammals of the Mesozoic or Triassic eras.

- Find another early mammal of that period (not the eomaia or repenomamus).
- Choose interesting facts that paleontologists know about that mammal.
- If possible, copy a picture of what the animal might look like.
- Prepare a short report about the animal and present it to your class.

PART 1
When with the Simple Past Tense
and Past Progressive

PART 2
While with the Simple Past Tense
and Past Progressive

Lesson (19)

World History: Ancient Egypt

■ CONTENT VOCABULARY

Look at the pictures. Do you know the words?

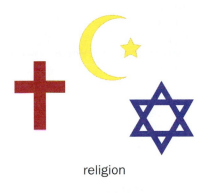

religion

a priest

a temple

to pray

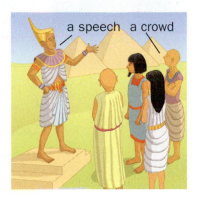

a speech   a crowd

Write the new words in your vocabulary journal.

■ THINK ABOUT IT

When you were younger, did anyone tell you to change what you like, where you live, or what you do? What happened? How did you feel? Discuss these questions with a partner.

■ GRAMMAR IN CONTENT

A Read and listen to the following passage about Akhenaton.

CD2,TR9

Akhenaton

In 1714, a French priest **was traveling** along the Nile **when** he **saw** the walls of an old city in the sand. Over 150 years later, an Egyptian woman **was walking** in the desert **when** she **found** hundreds of stone tablets. These two discoveries helped us learn about the life of Akhenaton.

Akhenaton lived in ancient Egypt over 3,000 years ago. **When** his father Amenhotep III **died,** Akhenaton **became** pharaoh. **When** Akhenaton **came** to the throne, Egyptians **were living** peaceful lives and **believed** in hundreds of gods. Akhenaton changed that. He changed Egypt's religion and told people there was only one god, Aton (the sun). Priests **were** angry **when** Akhenaton **closed** their temples and **took** away their power. **When** Akhenaton **died,** the priests **returned** to their old religion. Everyone forgot about him until the discovery of the tablets.

peaceful: calm, quiet   **a tablet:** a large, flat block of stone with writing on it

B Check (✔) *True* or *False.*

	True	False
1. An Egyptian woman found some stone tablets.	☐	☐
2. Akhenaton was a pharaoh.	☐	☐
3. Akhenaton closed the priests' temples.	☐	☐
4. The priests of the old gods did not like change.	☐	☐

When with the Simple Past Tense	
***When* + Clause in the Simple Past**	**Clause in the Simple Past**
When Amenhotep III **died,**	Akhenaton **became** pharaoh.

Note:

• Use *when* to show that one action followed another. Both clauses are in the simple past tense.

When with the Past Progressive	
***When* + Clause in the Simple Past**	**Clause in the Past Progressive**
When she **found** the tablets,	she **was walking** in the desert.

Note:

• Use *when* to show that one action interrupts a longer action. The shorter action is in the simple past.

C Complete each sentence with *when* to show an interrupted action in the past. Use the words in parentheses.

1. Amenhotep III _was planning_ (plan) more cities when he ___got___ (get) sick.

2. Akhenaton _____ (hunt) lions when his father

   _____ (die).

3. Akhenaton _____ (not think) about marriage when he

   _____ (meet) Nefertiti, his future wife.

4. Nefertiti _____ (expect) her first baby when Akhenaton

   _____ (marry) another woman.

5. Akhenaton _____ (hope) for a boy when Nefertiti

   _____ (give) birth to a baby girl.

D Complete the paragraph with the simple past or past progressive. Use the words in parentheses.

When I _____ (get) to the bus stop, a lot of people _____ (wait). The
          (1)   (2)
bus was late. After a long time, a bus _____ (come). When we _____ (pass)
                                        (3)   (4)
the history museum, I _____ (know) I was on the wrong bus. But I _____
                      (5)   (6)
(see) a poster for the Akhenaton exhibit, and I _____ (ask) the bus driver to stop.
                                                 (7)

■ **C O M M U N I C A T E**

E **PAIR WORK** Work with a classmate. Take turns asking and answering questions using the prompts below.

What was happening when . . .

1. . . . you came to class today?
2. . . . you had breakfast this morning?
3. . . . your instructor started the class?

■ GRAMMAR IN CONTENT

A Read and listen.

CD2,TR10

Akhenaton's Family

Rick: **While** I **was coming** to class this morning, I **was thinking** about Akhenaton's family. What were they like?

Dr. H: Well, Rick, **while** Akhenaton and Nefertiti **were ruling** Egypt, they gave their children lots of attention. They kissed and hugged their children, even in public. No pharaoh or queen of Egypt did that before.

Rick: Right. **While** I was **reading** my Egyptology book, I **noticed** a picture of the royal family. While Nefertiti **was holding** their daughters, Akhenaton **was kissing** one of them!

Dr. H: Yes, that's a really wonderful piece of art. The Amarna Period was a wonderful time in Egyptian history.

B Check (✔) *True* or *False*.

	True	False
1. Rick thought about Akhenaton's family while having breakfast.	☐	☐
2. Egyptian kings and queens always showed love of family in public.	☐	☐
3. Akhenaton loved his daughters very much.	☐	☐
4. The time that Akhenaton lived is called the Amarna Period.	☐	☐

While with the Past Progressive Tense	
While + Clause in the Past Progressive	Clause in the Simple Past
While I **was reading** a book about Akhenaton,	I **found** a great picture of him.
While + Clause in the Past Progressive	Clause in the Past Progressive
While I **was listening** to the instructor,	I **was taking** notes.

Notes:

• Use *while* with the clause in the past progressive (for the longer action).

• Also use *when* with the past progressive.

• The two clauses can be reversed: *I found a great picture of Akhenaton while I was reading a book about him.*

C Look at each of the following sentences. If you find no mistake in a sentence, write "correct" on the blank line after it. If you find a mistake, correct it.

1. While he ~~walked~~ *was walking* to the Temple of Amun-Ra, Nebtaui met one of his priests. _____

2. While Senmut prayed, he was waiting for Nebtaui. _____

3. When Akhenaton grew up, he learned about all the gods of Egypt. _____

4. While Nefertiti met Akhenaton, he was learning how to be a pharaoh. _____

5. In the second year of her marriage, Nefertiti was giving birth to a baby girl. _____

6. When Akhenaton died, the priests were planning to get back their power. _____

D Look at the pictures. Write a sentence for each picture using the words in parentheses. Use *while*, the past progressive, and the simple past in each sentence.

1. (walk / fall) _____ *While he was walking, he fell.* _____

2. (wake up / shine)

_____

3. (talk / work)

_____

4. (eat / play music)

_____

5. (paint / sit)

_____

■ **C O M M U N I C A T E**

E **PAIR WORK** **Work with a classmate. Take turns finishing the sentences below.**

1. While I was coming to class today . . .
2. While I was doing this lesson . . .
3. While I was going home last night . . .
4. When I was eating dinner last night . . .

Connection | Putting It Together

GRAMMAR AND VOCABULARY Imagine Akhenaton is the new pharaoh and you are an angry priest. Write a short journal entry about what was happening at that time. Use the grammar and vocabulary in this lesson.

PROJECT Perform a skit.

1. Work in groups of three.
2. Write a skit about Akhenaton, Nefertiti, and a priest.
3. Perform your skit for the class.

 INTERNET Go online. Search for information on Amarna, Akhenaton, Nefertiti, or Aton. Find out some interesting facts about the subject you choose. Tell your classmates what you found out.

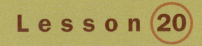

Lesson ⑳

Business:
Workplace Manners

■ CONTENT VOCABULARY

Look at the pictures. Do you know the words?

an interviewer

a résumé

a suit

an interview

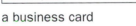

Jonathan Anders
Senior Editor
Thomson ELT

THOMSON
HEINLE

Thomson Heinle
25 Thomson Place
Boston, MA 02210

Tel (617) 555-0100   Fax (617) 555-0110
jonanders@thomson.com
www.elt.thomson.com
Thomson Learning Solutions

a business card

annoyed   embarrassed

Write the new words in your vocabulary journal.

■ THINK ABOUT IT

Do you have a job right now? If you do, do you have communication problems at work with the boss or colleagues? If you aren't working, do you know anybody who is working and is having these problems? Talk about this with some classmates.

■ GRAMMAR IN CONTENT

A Read and listen to this conversation between Abai and his English instructor, Ms. White.

CD2, TR11

Work Problems

Abai: I think I **should** go back to my country, Ms. White.

Ms. W: Why do you think you **ought to** do that, Abai?

Abai: I don't like working in the U.S. I can't make friends with my colleagues.

Ms. W: Don't you make small talk with your colleagues?

Abai: Not while I'm working.

Ms. W: Americans like to do that, Abai. You **shouldn't** remain silent if they're trying to make small talk with you.

Abai: And why did my boss get angry when I brought a beer to work for lunch?

Ms. W: Oh, no! You **mustn't** bring alcohol to the workplace. That's prohibited.

Abai: You **ought to** plan some lessons for the whole class on how to work in the U.S.

Ms. W: Actually, that's a great idea. I think I will.

to make small talk: chat about unimportant things

to prohibit: to not allow something, sometimes by order of law

B Check (✔) *True* or *False.*

	True	False
1. Americans like to make small talk while they work.	☐	☐
2. Americans make Abai angry.	☐	☐
3. Ms. White understands what the problem is.	☐	☐
4. Ms. White gave Abai's class some lessons on the American workplace.	☐	☐

Should, Ought To, Must Not

Subject	Should/ Ought To	Base Verb	Subject	Should not/Shouldn't Must not/Mustn't	Base Verb
I You He She It We They	should ought to	stay in the U.S.	I You He She It We They	should not/shouldn't must not/mustn't	leave the U.S.

C **Nabil is going for a job interview. He is asking his friend for advice. Complete the dialogues with *should, ought to, shouldn't,* or *mustn't.* Use the word in parentheses to write each question.**

1. **Nabil:** _____ *Should I* _____ (bring) extra résumés?

   John: Yes, _____ *you should* _____ . You _____ *ought to bring* _____ extra résumés.

2. **Nabil:** What _____ (wear)?

   John: You should wear a suit.

3. **Nabil:** When _____ (arrive)?

   John: You _____ at least 15 minutes before the interview.

4. **Nabil:** If I want to smoke, _____ (offer) a cigarette to the interviewer?

   John: You _____ smoke. It's illegal to smoke in an office.

5. **Nabil:** _____ (do) nothing except answer the interviewer's questions?

   John: You _____ ask questions about the company and about benefits.

6. **Nabil:** _____ (answer) questions about my personal life?

   John: No. For example, _____ questions about your marital status or religion.

D Read the situations below. Imagine you are a colleague. Write two sentences of advice, one negative, one affirmative. Use *should/shouldn't, ought to,* or *mustn't* and the verbs in parentheses.

> Can you tell me what I did wrong? All I did was tell the boss I like his toupee. He looked at me so strangely—and he never answered my question.

1. (ask) _You shouldn't ask questions that may embarrass people._

2. (avoid) _You ought to avoid questions that are too personal._

> I don't understand my American boss. Why does he get upset with me? I come to work late a couple of times a week. So what? I can stay late if he wants. What am I doing that's so terrible?

3. (arrive) _____

4. (ask) _____

> The boss is too strict. I was eating some popcorn and drinking a soda while working at the computer. She told me never to do that again. What's that all about?

5. (eat or drink) _____

6. (keep) _____

> I'm getting friendly with some American men at work. I invited those men to my home for dinner a few times, but they never accepted. When I see their wives at the office, they don't act friendly to me. Am I doing something wrong?

7. (invite) _____

8. (include) _____

> My boss isn't very nice. For example, yesterday I went to the employee lounge. Nobody was there, so I had a cigarette. Then, my boss came in and shouted at me. What was the problem? I don't understand.

9. (smoke) _____

10. (go outside) _____

> I'm upset with the boss. I was trying to get his attention, so I snapped my fingers. The boss turned to me and looked very annoyed. He didn't come over. Did I do something wrong? How do you get somebody's attention?

11. (snap) _____

12. (say) _____

■ COMMUNICATE

E **GROUP WORK** Work with two or three classmates. Think about where you work or study. What are some things you and others should, shouldn't, and mustn't do there?

> I work in a library. People mustn't talk loud there.

F **WRITE** Write about the differences between two cultures you know. Use *should*, *shouldn't*, and *mustn't*.

PART TWO	*Have To, Must, Had To*

■ GRAMMAR IN CONTENT

CD2,TR12

A Read and listen to this conversation between colleagues. They work in the same department at the same company. They are engaged to be married.

> **Sam:** So, did you tell the boss that we're getting married?
>
> **Noor:** No, we **don't have to** tell him that. It'll be bad for us if we do.
>
> **Sam:** Why? What do you mean?
>
> **Noor:** The company says that two employees in the same department **have to** tell the company if they're getting married. One of them **must** transfer to another department if there's an opening—or leave the company.
>
> **Sam:** What? But why **do** we **have to** do that?
>
> **Noor:** They don't want married couples working in the same department. It's bad for business. If we don't want to transfer or leave the company, we **must** keep our marriage a secret. Jenny and Fabio in Accounting **had** to tell their boss because too many people knew their plans. Jenny lost her job!
>
> **Sam:** Okay, we'll **have to** keep our marriage a secret if we want to continue working together.

transfer: to move from one place to another

B Check (✔) *True* or *False*.

	True	False
1. Sam and Noor got married recently.	☐	☐
2. Noor knows more about company rules than Sam does.	☐	☐
3. The company doesn't want married couples working together.	☐	☐
4. Sam is going to tell his boss about their plans.	☐	☐

Must/Have To; Don't/Doesn't Have To; Had To/Didn't Have To

Subject	Must/ Have To	Base Verb	Subject	Don't/Doesn't Have To	Base Verb
I You We They	must have to had to	tell the truth.	I You We They	don't have to didn't have to	tell the truth.
He She It	must has to had to	be ready.	He She	doesn't have to didn't have to	be ready.

Notes:

- *must* and *have to* = it's necessary; *had to* = it was necessary

  don't have to = it's not necessary; *didn't have to* = it wasn't necessary

- Use *must* in questions and short answers: *Must* + subject + base verb . . . ? Example: **Must they tell** the boss their wedding plans? Yes, **they must.** / No, **they don't have to.**

- Use *don't/doesn't have to* in negatives.

- Use *have to* in questions and short answers: *Do/Does/Did* + subject + base verb...?

  Does Sam have to tell his boss he's marrying Noor? Yes, **he does.** / No, **he doesn't.**

  Did Noor have to find another job? Yes, **she did.** / No, **she didn't.**

C (Circle) the best choice to complete each sentence.

1. **A:** Are you taking a vacation day tomorrow?
   B: Yes, I am. I (have to / has to) tell my boss. She (must / doesn't have to) put it on my timesheet.

2. **A:** (Do you must / Do you have to) tell the boss why you're taking a personal day?
   B: No, you (mustn't / don't have to) explain to the boss why you're taking a personal day.

3. **A:** (Do Americans must / Must Americans) shake hands every day when they see their coworkers?
   B: No, (they mustn't / they don't).

4. **A:** In the United States, a person (doesn't have to be / must be) 16 to work full time, right?
   B: The minimum age to work full time is 16.

5. **A:** I understand that employees must tell the boss what their religion is.
   B: Not in the United States. Employees (don't have to / doesn't have to) tell the boss what their religion is.

6. **A:** If it's really busy at work, must you work overtime?
   B: No, you (don't have to / mustn't), but it's a good thing if you do.

D Complete the questions and short answers about Americans at work.
Use *must/have to* and *don't have to.*

1. **Q:** _____Do_____ you _____have to_____ say "Sir" or "Ma'am" when speaking to the boss?

   A: No, _____you don't_____. That title is too formal for most Americans.

2. **Q:** _____ employees always call in sick if they are too sick to go to work?

   A: Yes, _____.

3. **Q:** _____ a man _____ earn more money than his wife?

   A: No, _____. But for some men, it's difficult to accept that possibility.

4. **Q:** _____ bosses _____ give employees bonuses at Christmastime?

   A: No, _____, but it's a nice thing to do.

5. **Q:** _____ you wear a suit if the boss tells you to?

   A: Yes, _____. Your employer has the right to tell you to dress in a suit.

6. **Q:** _____ you _____ keep eye contact with somebody who's talking to you?

   A: Yes, _____. It shows respect and interest.

E Complete the sentences about things that were necessary or not necessary to do in the past. Use *had to* or *didn't have to* and a verb.

1. When Cynthia got the flu, she _____. She didn't want to infect her coworkers.

2. The doctor said that Cynthia _____ to her office. There was no medicine the doctor could give her.

3. When Paul applied for a job with the government, he _____ a drug test.

4. Roger _____ lunch with his coworkers, but he wanted to be friendly.

5. The boss understood why Nancy couldn't stay late to finish a special job. He knew that she _____ at home with her children because her husband works nights.

6. When my car broke down, you _____ me a ride home. But you did, and that was very kind of you. Thanks.

■ C O M M U N I C A T E

F **PAIR WORK** Talk about where you work or study. What do you have to do, be, or have in order to be successful?

G **WRITE** Write about a job you had or a school you went to in the past. Write about things you had to do or didn't have to do.

Connection | Putting It Together

GRAMMAR AND VOCABULARY Work with two or three classmates. Imagine you are managers. You notice that many of the office workers are not acting friendly with one another. You don't know why. Make a list of what you should do to find out the problem and solve it. Make another list of what you should not or must not do. Tell the class your ideas.

PROJECT Create a workplace utopia.

1. Work with two or three classmates. You're going to plan a perfect workplace.
2. Think about where you work or study. Write down things you like and don't like about it.
3. Make a list of words that describe what your utopian place is like.
4. Present your decisions to the class.

 INTERNET Go online. Search for sites that give advice about job interviews. Find out what you should and shouldn't do. Report back to your classmates.

A Complete the conversation between two tenants in an apartment building. Gene is an old tenant, and Raj is a new tenant from India. Use the verbs in parentheses. Think of words to put in the other blanks.

Raj: Hi Gene! We're having a barbecue next week.

Gene: That's great! _____ (1) you (barbecue) _____ (2) a lot _____ (3) you (live) _____ (4) in your country, Raj?

Raj: Yes, we _____ (5) .

Gene: So which park _____ (6) you (choose) _____ (7) for the barbecue?

Raj: Park? No park. The balcony of our apartment is fine. I (put) _____ (8) a new barbecue grill out there last weekend.

Gene: What? You _____ (9) a barbecue on your balcony!

Raj: Why?

Gene: A few years _____ (10) , _____ (11) a tenant in another building (have) _____ (12) a barbecue on his balcony, he (start) _____ (13) a fire. The fire (burn) _____ (14) half the building. _____ (15) that terrible fire happened, we (have) _____ (16) any laws against cooking on balconies, but _____ (17) the fire, the city government (pass) _____ (18) a new law against it. Anyway, you _____ (19) barbecue on your balcony. It's not allowed.

Raj: Okay, Gene. Thanks for the advice.

B You're Dr. Doright. Your patients are asking you to help them. Read their stories and tell them what to do. Use the verbs in parentheses. Fill in all the other blanks.

Patient: _____ (1) I (buy) _____ (2) some things in the drugstore, I (find) _____ (3) a new herbal medicine to stop arthritis pain. But _____ (4) I (take) _____ (5) the new medicine, I (begin) _____ (6) to feel sick.

Doctor: You _____(7)_____ take new medicines _____(8)_____ you check with me.

_____(9)_____ you (take) _____(10)_____ your heart medicine _____(11)_____ you (try)

_____(12)_____ that new medicine?

Patient: Yes, I _____(13)_____.

Doctor: You _____(14)_____ be very careful about mixing some medicines. That can

be dangerous.

Doctor: Hi, Jackie. Let me see your hand. Hmm . . . I think this is a snake bite.

When _____(15)_____ this (happen) _____(16)_____?

Jackie: Early this morning.

Doctor: Jackie, what _____(17)_____ you (do) _____(18)_____ _____(19)_____ this happened?

Jackie: I (move) _____(20)_____ _____(21)_____ some big rocks in the backyard.

Doctor: _____(22)_____ something (bite) _____(23)_____ you _____(24)_____ you (move)

_____(25)_____ one of those rocks?

Jackie: Yes.

Doctor: There aren't any poisonous snakes in this area, so that's good. We

(worry) _____(26)_____ about that. I'll clean the bite and put on a bandage.

Jackie: Thank you, Doctor.

LEARNER LOG Check (✔) *Yes* or *I Need More Practice.*

Lesson	I Can Use . . .	Yes	I Need More Practice
16	The Simple Past Tense with Regular Verbs in Statements and *Yes/No* Questions and Short Answers		
17	The Simple Past Tense with Irregular Verbs in Statements, Information Questions, and *Before* and *After*		
18	The Past Progressive Tense in Statements and Questions		
19	The Simple Past and Past Progressive Tenses with *When* and *While*		
20	*Should, Shouldn't,* and *Ought To* for Advice, *Mustn't* for Prohibition, and *Must, Have To,* and *Don't Have To* for Necessity		

PART 1
Can, May for Permission;
Can, Could, Would for Requests

PART 2
Want, Would Like for Desires

Lesson 21

Business: The Hospitality Industry

■ CONTENT VOCABULARY

Look at the pictures. Do you know the words?

HOTEL RECEPTION
a guest
a desk clerk
registration desk

to make a reservation

check in

check out

TRAVEL
a travel agent
a customer
brochures
a travel agency

a cruise ship

Write the new words in your vocabulary journal.

■ THINK ABOUT IT

Have you ever been in a hotel? How do you get a room in a hotel? What do guests often ask for? What do desk clerks usually ask? Discuss your answers with your classmates.

■ **GRAMMAR IN CONTENT**

CD2,TR13

A **Read and listen.**

A Reservation for Two

Clerk: Hotel of the Americas. **May** I help you?

Gigi: Yes, please. **Can** I make a reservation for next weekend?

Clerk: Certainly, ma'am.

Gigi: **Can** I have a nonsmoking room?

Clerk: No problem. **May** I have your name, please?

Gigi: It's Gigi Sablier.

Clerk: **Would** you spell the last name, please?

Gigi: S as in "Sam" – A – B as in "boy" – L – I – E – R. Oh, one more thing. **Can** my dog stay in the hotel?

Clerk: Hmm . . . I'm not sure, Ms. Sablier. I'm new here. **Could** you hold, please?

Gigi: Okay.

Clerk: Thank you for holding. Yes, your dog **can** stay in the hotel.

to hold: to wait for someone on the phone

B **Check (✔) *True, False,* or *Don't Know.***

	True	False	Don't Know
1. Gigi wants a reservation for five nights.	☐	☐	☐
2. Gigi says "S as in 'Sam'" and "B as in 'boy'" to make sure the clerk understands her.	☐	☐	☐
3. Gigi does not want to be put on hold.	☐	☐	☐
4. The hotel allows guests to bring pets.	☐	☐	☐

***Can, May* for Permission: Statements**					
Affirmative			**Negative**		
Subject	***Can / May***		**Subject**	***Cannot / May not***	
You	can may	stay here.	You	cannot / can't may not	go there.

Notes:

• Use *can* and *may* to tell someone it's okay to do something.

• *Can* is informal. *May* is more formal. *Could* is also used in many situations.

Can, May for Permission: Yes/No Questions

			Short Answers
Can			Ok.
Could	I	stay here (, please)?	Sure.
May			Yes, of course.
			No, sorry.
			I'm afraid not.

Can, Could, Would for Requests

			Short Answers
Can			Ok.
Could	you	call the front desk (, please)?	Sure.
Would			Yes, of course.
			No, sorry. I'm too busy.

Notes:

- Use *can*, *could*, and *would* to ask someone to do something.
- *Would* is only used with *you* to make a request. With *can* and *could* use any of the pronouns.
- *Can* is informal. *Could* and *would* are more polite and formal.

C **Read the questions. Decide if they are asking for permission or making a request. Check (✔) the appropriate box.**

	Permission	Request
1. Can I make a reservation for next weekend?	☐	☐
2. Can I pay for the room by credit card?	☐	☐
3. May I have your name, please?	☐	☐
4. Would you spell the last name, please?	☐	☐
5. Could I use your phone, please?	☐	☐
6. Can my dog stay in the hotel?	☐	☐
7. Could you check on that too, please?	☐	☐

D **Complete the questions with the phrases in the box.**

May I borrow	~~Can I stay~~	Can we leave	Would you sign
May I help	Could you take	Could I have	Could you fill out

1. **Customer:** _____ Can I stay _____ at this hotel?

   Agent: Sorry. That hotel is full.

2. **Manager:** _____ your time sheet?

   Desk clerk: Sure.

3. **Woman:** _____ the rental car at the hotel?

   Travel agent: Sorry, you must bring it back to the airport.

4. **Desk clerk:** _____ the receipt here please?

   Man: Of course. _____ your pen?

5. **Woman:** _____ my bags to the room please?

   Desk clerk: Yes, ma'am.

6. **Desk clerk:** _____ the day off tomorrow?

   Manager: Sorry, it's a busy day.

7. **Manager:** _____ you?

   Customer: Yes, please. Where's the elevator?

E Listen to this interview between a reporter and a person from the Tourism and Hospitality Association. Recreate the interview using *can, may, could,* and *would* when appropriate with the verbs in parentheses.

CD2,TR14

Reporter: _____*Can I ask*_____ (ask) you a few questions about the hospitality
              (1)
industry, Mr. Hwang?

Hwang: Certainly.

Reporter: _____ (tell) me how many jobs there are in
              (2)
this industry?

Hwang: Thousands and thousands of jobs! _____ (send) you a
                                             (3)
complete list of all the kinds of jobs available?

Reporter: Yes, please. _____ (send) it to my office?
                           (4)
That _____ (be) very interesting to see.
      (5)
_____ (ask) you what salaries are like in
(6)
the industry?

Hwang: Just like in every industry, the more education or training you

have, the higher your salary can be.

■ COMMUNICATE

F PAIR WORK Work with a classmate. Imagine Student A is checking into a hotel. Student B is the registration clerk. Use the phrases below to create a conversation.

Could you recommend a restaurant near the hotel?

Sure. There's a great restaurant just around the corner.

Asking for Permission

1. park my car in this lot
2. see your passport please
3. pay with a traveler's check
4. change rooms for one that is more quiet

Making Requests

5. cancel our hotel reservation for us
6. send us a refund
7. give us a different rental car
8. book us a three-day cruise

PART TWO | *Want, Would Like* for Desires

■ GRAMMAR IN CONTENT

CD2, TR15

A Read and listen.

Asking for a Loan

Bank Manager:	So, you're interested in opening a small hotel.
Harry:	Yes, we **would like** to get a loan, please.
Bank Manager:	How much money **would** you **like**?
Harry:	$70,000.
Tillie:	No, Harry. I think we **want** more than that.
Harry:	Really?
Tillie:	Yes, we want $90,000.
Harry:	Oh, yes. I'm sorry, Mr. Gold. We**'d like** $90,000.
Bank Manager:	**Would** you **like** a fixed interest rate?
Harry:	**Do** you **want** a fixed rate, Tillie?
Tillie:	Yes, we**'d like** a fixed rate, please.
Bank Manager:	Great. Could you fill out these forms, please? **Would you like** a cup of coffee?
Harry:	That would be nice. Thanks.

a loan: a sum of money borrowed at a rate of interest

a fixed rate: an interest rate that remains the same for the length of the loan

	True	False
1. Harry and Tillie have a hotel.	☐	☐
2. Harry and Tillie want a loan.	☐	☐
3. Harry and Tillie agree on the size of the loan they need.	☐	☐
4. Mr. Gold has good manners.	☐	☐

Statements with *Want* and *Would Like*

I You	want	
He She	doesn't want	a loan.
We They	would like	

Notes:

- *Want* is a "strong" verb. There is power in the word. In a formal situation, it may sound impolite.
- *Would like* is not as strong as *want.* The meaning is the same, but the phrase is more polite.
- The contraction for *would* is *'d.* Examples: *I'd, you'd, he'd, she'd, we'd, they'd.*
- When *would like = want,* only use *don't/doesn't want* for the negative: *We **would like** round-trip tickets. / We **don't want** one-way tickets.*

Questions with *Want* and *Would Like*

Question		Answer
Do you want	a loan?	Yes, please.
Would you like		No, thanks.

Note:

Use *Do you want* and *Would you like* in an informal situation. Use *Would you like* in formal situations.

C Read the dialogues. Change the desires so they are more polite.

1. **Hotel clerk:** Good morning.

   Guest: I ~~want~~ *would like* some help.

2. **Server:** Do you want more coffee?

   Customer: Yes, please. I want cream and sugar too.

3. **Passenger:** I'm not comfortable.

   Flight attendant: Do you want a pillow?

4. **Car rental agent:** Do you want the car for one week?

   Customer: Yes, please.

5. **Guest:** I want a taxi.

   Hotel clerk: Okay, I'll call for one.

D Look at each picture. Complete each statement or question using *would like* or *want*.

Customer: _____*I'd like*_____ the steak please.
(1)

Waiter: _____ something to drink?
(2)

Customer: _____ coffee, please.
(3)

Travel agent: _____ to see
(4)
the brochure?

Client: Yes, please.

Mom: _____ some ice-cream?
(5)

Child: _____ chocolate, please.
(6)

Agent: Where would you like to stay?

Customer: _____ a big hotel. We like
(7)
staying at smaller hotels.

Husband: _____ to go to Egypt
(8)
or Italy?

Wife: _____ to go to Italy. We went
(9)
there last year. I _____ to
(10)
go to Egypt.

■ **COMMUNICATE**

E **GROUP WORK** Discuss these questions in groups.

1. Would you like to start your own business?
2. What business would you like to have?
3. What would you like to sell or do?
4. Where would you like your business to be?

GRAMMAR AND VOCABULARY Work in pairs. Look at the following situations. Create a dialogue for each one. Ask for permission, make a request, or mention a desire. Use the grammar and vocabulary from the lesson.

- You're the hotel desk clerk. A guest is returning. She's carrying too many packages and some are ready to fall to the floor.
- You're a hotel desk clerk. A guest is upset. The guest is telling you that the person in the next room keeps playing music too loud.
- You and a friend are in the airport waiting for your plane. You're thirsty and decide to get a soda. You think your friend may be thirsty, too.
- You're in a travel agency, looking at a brochure about cruises. One cruise looks interesting, but you don't know where the ship stops. You see that one of the agents isn't busy.
- You're a customs agent at the airport. Passengers are coming past you with their luggage. You want to look inside a passenger's suitcase.

PROJECT Create a tourism advertisement.

1. Work with a group of classmates.
2. Choose a town or city your group knows well. Imagine that you all work for the tourist information office.
3. Prepare a short advertisement to attract tourists to the town or city you chose. You might want to include information about the following:

   - things to do
   - places to visit
   - good restaurants and nightlife

4. Present your advertisement to your class.

 INTERNET Go online. Use the keywords "schools of hospitality" or "schools of hotel management" and find a community college, university, or programs at a vocational school. Find out the following:

- types of programs the school offers
- types of courses the programs include
- length of program
- cost of tuition
- types of degrees or certificates offered

Academic Success: The Internet

■ CONTENT VOCABULARY

Look at the pictures. Do you know the words?

a website

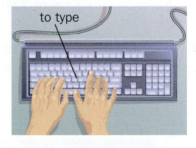
to search
select

to type
to click

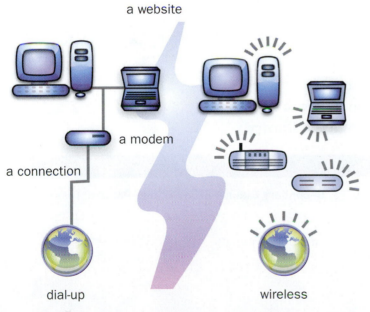

a modem

a connection

dial-up

wireless

Write the new words in your vocabulary journal.

■ THINK ABOUT IT

Do you use the Internet? What do you use the Internet for? Discuss your answers with a classmate.

■ GRAMMAR IN CONTENT

CD2, TR16

A Read and listen.

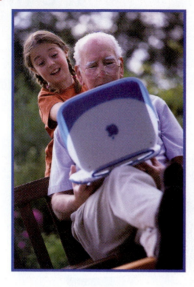

You're Never Too Old to Learn

Grandpa: Hey, Jenny. What are you doing?

Jenny: I'm doing some research on the Internet.

Grandpa: How does that work?

Jenny: Well, **if** you **want** information quickly, you **go** to a search engine. Look, I'll show you. **When** you type the keywords here, you **hit** "Enter."

Grandpa: Wow! Look at all the things that came up.

Jenny: Amazing, isn't it? **If** I **don't find** a good link, I **try** a different one.

Grandpa: You know, **if** I **want** some information, I usually **go** to the library. I guess that's quite old-fashioned now.

old-fashioned: no longer in common use

B Check (✔) *True* or *False*.

	True	False
1. Jenny is using the Internet.	☐	☐
2. Jenny shows her grandfather how to find information by clicking on a link to a website.	☐	☐
3. Jenny's grandfather doesn't go to the library.	☐	☐

Factual Conditional Statements

If Clause in the Simple Present Tense	Secondary Clause in the Simple Present Tense
If When I **want** information quickly,	I **go** to the Internet.

Notes:

• Use real conditionals to talk about facts and routines. Examples: *If you don't have a computer, you can't use the Internet. If I arrive at school early, I go to the computer lab.*

• When you begin your statement with the *if* clause, put a comma (,) after that clause.

• Factual conditionals can start with the secondary clause: Example: *I go to the Web when I want information quickly.*

C Complete the conditional sentences using the words in parentheses and *if*.

1. (your computer / stops working) _If your computer stops working_, turn it off, and then turn it back on.

2. Find a new Internet service provider (your connection / be bad) _____.

3. (you / see a padlock icon) _____, the personal information you fill in there is safe.

4. (you / not get many links) _____, use different keywords.

5. People on other computers can see you (you / use a webcam) _____.

6. (a URL / has ".edu" at the end) _____, it is a college website.

7. (a URL /has ".gov" at the end) _____, it is a government website.

D Complete the statements with your own ideas.

1. When I get too much homework, _____.

2. If my computer doesn't work, _____.

3. If a cell phone rings in class, _____.

4. When I get a good grade, _____.

5. If I go to the mall, _____.

■ **C O M M U N I C A T E**

E **PAIR WORK** Find out what your partner wrote for exercise D.

■ GRAMMAR IN CONTENT

A Read and listen.

CD2,TR17

A Modern Shopper

Reporter:	**What do** you **do if** you **feel** stressed?
Pavel:	If I feel stressed, I shop online.
Reporter:	**If** you **go** to the mall, **do** you **feel** stressed?
Pavel:	Absolutely! I feel much less stress if I don't go to the mall.
Reporter:	**Why do** you **get** stressed **if** you **go** to the mall?
Pavel:	Parking is always a problem, there are too many people, and it takes so much time.
Reporter:	**Do** you **buy** more things **if** you **shop** online?
Pavel:	Yes, I do—because it's easier.

B Check (✔) *True* or *False*.

	True	False
1. Pavel feels less stress shopping online than shopping at the mall.	☐	☐
2. He doesn't go to the mall because he doesn't have a car.	☐	☐
3. Pavel mentions three reasons that malls make him feel stressed.	☐	☐
4. Shopping online affects how many purchases he makes.	☐	☐

Factual Conditional Questions	
If Clause in the Simple Present Tense	**Secondary Clause in Question Form**
When/If you shop at the mall,	do you feel stressed?
Secondary Clause in Question Form	**If Clause in the Simple Present Tense**
Do you feel stressed	when/if you shop at the mall?

Notes:

• When you begin a real conditional question with the *if* clause, put a comma after it.

• When you begin a real conditional question with the secondary clause, don't put a comma after it.

C Complete the dialogues using the words in parentheses.

1. (Why / people get dial-up) (broadband is quicker)

   Customer: _Why do people get dial-up if broadband is quicker_ ?

   Sales associate: Dial-up is cheaper.

2. (I choose dial-up) (get a modem)

   Customer: _____?

   Sales associate: Yes, you do.

3. (Who / I call) (my Internet connection not work)

   Customer: _____?

   Sales associate: We have a 24-hour helpline you can call.

4. (buy this laptop) (get wireless Internet)

   Customer: _____?

   Sales associate: No, you don't.

5. (wireless work) (use it on a train)

   Customer: _____?

   Sales associate: Sometimes it does, but not always.

■ **C O M M U N I C A T E**

D **GROUP WORK** Interview four classmates. Ask each person a *Yes/No* question and a conditional question about their use of computers.

Do you have a computer?

If you use the Internet, what do you use it for?

Yes, I do.

I usually practice my English in chat rooms if I'm on the Internet.

GRAMMAR AND VOCABULARY Work with a classmate. One of you look only at this page (Classmate A). The other should look only at page 236 (Classmate B). Classmate A reads the beginnings of the four conditional sentences to the other. Classmate B chooses the best way to finish each sentence and tells you. Then reverse what you did for the next four sentences.

Classmate A:

1. I can't do a search on the Internet . . .
2. If I open an e-mail from an unknown sender, . . .
3. If a company doesn't have a website, . . .
4. All the employees in a company can communicate very fast . . .

5. a. it isn't hard to learn computer science.
   b. it's hard to learn computer science.
6. a. can receive documents quickly.
   b. can't receive documents quickly.
7. a. if they use information technology a lot.
   b. if they use computers a lot.
8. a. it hires a Web designer.
   b. it hires a computer programmer.

Classsmate B:

1. a. if my Internet connection is okay.
   b. if my Internet connection is broken.
2. a. I may infect my computer with a virus.
   b. I shouldn't answer it.
3. a. it does less business than companies with one.
   b. it can have a website.
4. a. if they have internal e-mail.
   b. if they have the Internet.

5. If you aren't good in mathematics, . . .
6. Without a computer or fax machine, people . . .
7. People know more about other cultures now than ever before . . .
8. If a company needs to have a website, . . .

 INTERNET PROJECT Go online and prepare a presentation. Work with one or two classmates. Research one of the following subjects on the Internet:

- a school (vocational or college) that offers a degree in Information Technology (IT)
- a company that designs and maintains Web sites
- a company that sells IT hardware and software

Nursing:
Being an LPN

■ CONTENT VOCABULARY

Look at the pictures. Do you know the words?

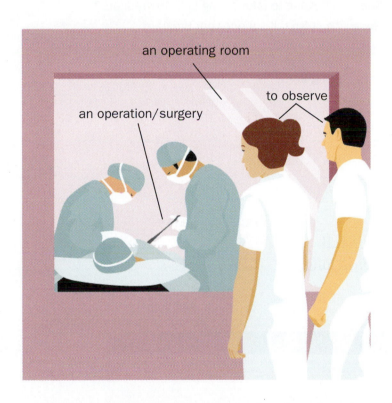

an operating room

to observe

an operation/surgery

a nurse

a doctor

a patient

a hospital ward

a uniform

Write the new words in your vocabulary journal.

■ THINK ABOUT IT

What are your plans when you finish college? What job would you like to have? Discuss your answers with your classmates.

■ GRAMMAR IN CONTENT

A Read and listen.

CD2,TR18

Becoming an LPN

Sue:	What **are** you **going to do** this fall?
Rosa:	**I'm going to go** back to college.
Sue:	Good for you! What are you **going to study?**
Rosa:	Licensed practical nursing.
Sue:	**Are** you **going to be** an LPN?
Rosa:	Yes, I **am.**
Sue:	**Is** it **going to take** a long time to graduate?
Rosa:	No, it **isn't.** It's a one-year program.
Sue:	Well, I'm really proud of you. Oh goodness, look at those dark clouds. We should go inside. I think **it's going to** rain.

LPN: Licensed Practical Nurse

B Check (✔) *True* or *False.*

	True	False
1. Sue is going to do office work this fall.	☐	☐
2. The course is going to be two years long.	☐	☐
3. It's going to rain.	☐	☐

Be Going To in Statements			
Subject	***Be Going To***	**Verb**	
I	am going to am not going to	be	a licensed practical nurse.
He She	is going to isn't going to	have	clinical classes in a hospital.
We You They	are going to aren't going to	take	one year to finish the program.
It	is going to	rain.	

Notes:

- Use *be going to* for set plans in the future. Example: *I'm going to be an LPN.*
- Use *be going to* to make predictions about the near future. *You're going to like the LPN program.*
- Use *be going to* when you expect something to happen. *Be careful! You're going to hurt yourself.*
- In speaking, *going to* is often pronounced "gonna."

Be Going To in Yes/No and Information Questions

	Subject	*Be Going To*	Base Verb		Short Answer
Am	I				Yes, I am.
Is	she	going to	take	a class next year?	No, she isn't.
Are	they				Yes, they are.

	Be	Subject	*Going To*	Base Verb	
What	am	I	going to	do	next year?
Where	is	she			
		he	going to	study	nursing?
When	are	they			
How long	is	it	going to	take?	

C Complete Rosa's journal entry. Use *be going to* and the verbs in parentheses.

November 3rd

Tomorrow, the class _____ (go) to the hospital.
                                    (1)

We _____ (not work) with patients. We _____
        (2)   (3)

(observe) the doctors. On Thursday, I _____ (start)
                                                          (4)

my first clinical class. I _____ (practice) being
                                  (5)

a nurse. I'm really nervous. Luckily, Sue _____ (be)
                                                              (6)

there too.

D Look at the following pictures. Write questions and answers. Use the words in parentheses and *be going to.*

1. **Q:** (she / buy a textbook) _Is she going to buy a textbook?_

   A: _____

You have one hour. Please begin.

2. **Q:** (what / he / do) _____

   _____

   A: _____

   _____

JUNE

Sun	Mon	Tue	Wed	Thu	Fri	Sat
			1	2	3	4
5	6	7	8	9	10	11
12	13	14	15	16	17	18
19	20	21	22	23	(24) Graduation day!	25
26	27	28	29	30		

3. **Q:** (when / he / graduate) _____

   _____

   A: _____

   _____

4. **Q:** (be / put on / pajamas) _____

   _____

   A: _____

5. **Q:** (what / she / do) _____

   _____

   A: _____

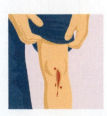

6. **Q:** (she / need / a bandage) _____

   _____

   A: _____

7. **Q:** (feel / pain / during the surgery) _____

_____

A: _____

8. **Q:** (help the patient / stand up) _____

_____

A: _____

■ COMMUNICATE

E Student A looks at the information on this page. Student B looks at the information on page **237**. Ask and answer questions to find out the information. Use *be going to.*

 What's he doing in 5 minutes?

 He's going to check on a patient.

Student A

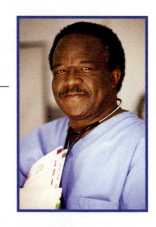

In 5 minutes: 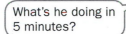 _check on a patient_

At midday: have quick lunch with _____

_____: study at home

Next Tuesday: go to yoga class

_____: run a marathon

Next year: ask for a pay raise

F **WRITE** Write about your plans and predictions for after you finish college.

After I finish my studies, I'm going to prepare for the state boards, the special exam I'm going to have to take to get my LPN license. They're going to give the exam in three months, so I'm going to study very hard until then.

■ GRAMMAR IN CONTENT

A Read and listen.

CD2,TR19

Making a Date

Ed: What **are** you **doing** tomorrow?

Sue: I**'m studying** for the state boards to get my LPN license.

Ed: What about the next day?

Sue: I**'m studying** then, too.

Ed: When **are** you **not studying?**

Sue: I**'m not studying** on the 28th. That's when I**'m taking** the state boards!

B Check (✔) *True* or *False.*

	True	False
1. Sue has an LPN license.	☐	☐
2. Sue is busy.	☐	☐
3. Sue doesn't have a test on the 28th.	☐	☐

The Future with the Present Progressive

Statements	Questions
I**'m helping** the patients this afternoon. He**'s not working** next Monday.	**Are** you **working** tomorrow? **Is** the nurse **coming** soon? **When** are you **going** to the hospital? **What** are you **doing** for lunch?

Notes:

• Use the present progressive for future plans that are definite. It is an alternative to *be going to.*

• But don't use the present progressive for predictions. NOT: ~~I'm being a nurse next year.~~

• Use future time expressions. Examples: *tomorrow / next week / soon / later*

• For more information on how to form the present progressive, see Lesson 9.

C Rosa is studying to be an LPN. Today is the 1ˢᵗ. Look at her calendar. Write a paragraph about her plans. Use the present progressive and the verbs in the box.

Tuesday	Wednesday	Thursday	Friday	Saturday
30 ✗	1	2 City Memorial Hospital – observation	3 Lunch with advisor Class presentations	4 Apartment move
7	8 Study for exam all day	9 final exam	10 San Diego– 8:10 flight	11 Sister's wedding

take   meet   fly   go   give   observe   study   move   not do

Rosa has a busy few weeks coming up. Tomorrow, she is observing
at the City Memorial Hospital.

D **PAIR WORK** Ask and answer questions about Rosa's schedule in exercise C. Use the present progressive.

E Look at the e-mail. There are 8 mistakes using *be going to* or the present progressive.

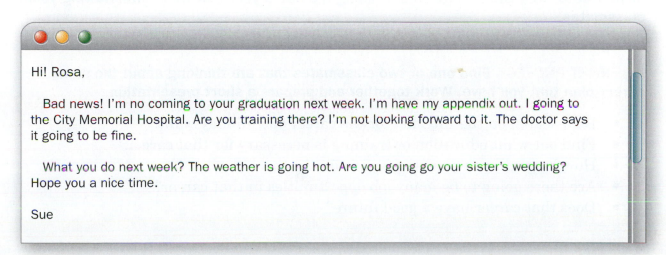

Hi! Rosa,

Bad news! I'm no coming to your graduation next week. I'm have my appendix out. I going to the City Memorial Hospital. Are you training there? I'm not looking forward to it. The doctor says it going to be fine.

What you do next week? The weather is going hot. Are you going go your sister's wedding? Hope you a nice time.

Sue

F **PAIR WORK** What plans do you have after you finish class today? Tell your partner.

What are you doing after class?

Why are you going home?

I'm going home.

I'm going to make dinner for my friend.

Connection | Putting It Together

GRAMMAR AND VOCABULARY Talk to your classmates. Find people who are and are not going to do the following things. Ask them questions and take notes about their answers. Use the grammar and vocabulary from the lesson.

Are you going to work as a nurse?

No, I'm going to be an engineer.

- stay home tonight
- see some friends this evening
- go to any parties soon
- move in the near future

- talk to a career counselor
- get an associate's/a bachelor's/a master's degree
- enter a vocational program
- work in business or the health field

In your notebook, write sentences by using the notes you took while interviewing your classmates.

 INTERNET PROJECT Find one or two classmates that are thinking about the same career plan that you have. Work together and prepare a short presentation.

- Do a search on the Internet for the career you all may want.
- Find out what education or training is necessary for that career.
- How long will you need to prepare for the career?
- Are there going to be many job opportunities in that career?
- Does that career have a good future?

Literature:
Science Fiction

■ CONTENT VOCABULARY

Look at the pictures. Do you know the words?

 the surface

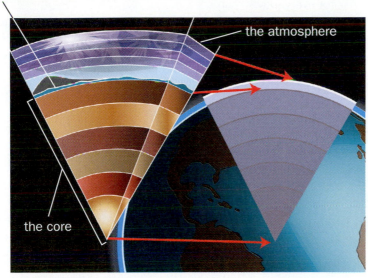

the atmosphere

the core

natural resources

to dig

to breathe

to plant

Write the new words in your vocabulary journal.

■ THINK ABOUT IT

What do you think will happen to our planet in the future? Do you think Earth's future looks good? Why or why not? Discuss these questions with your class.

■ **GRAMMAR IN CONTENT**

A Read and listen.

CD2,TR20

colonizing: sending people to live in another place while still governing them from home

Terraforming

What will the future **be** like? **Will it be** better than today? **Will it be** worse? Many science fiction writers write about the future. They base their ideas on scientific fact. Their ideas often predict the future. For example, Olaf Stapledon wrote a story about the planet Venus. At the end of the story, Venus was made to look more like Earth—a process called terraforming.

What is terraforming? Terraforming means making a planet more like Earth. In that way, plants, animals, and humans can live on that planet. Some scientists think new technologies **will make** this dream come true. They predict that many human beings **will need** to leave Earth because we **will not have** enough resources for everybody.

Today, there is a lot of talk about colonizing other planets. In 2012, the United States **will send** someone to Mars. **Will** scientists **be able to terraform** Mars in the future? Maybe, but it **won't happen** overnight. It **will** probably **take** many years.

B Check (✔) *True* or *False*.

	True	False
1. Science fiction writers use only their imagination to predict the future.	☐	☐
2. People will be able to live on other planets if they can terraform them.	☐	☐
3. Some scientists think that everybody will leave Earth one day.	☐	☐
4. Terraforming a planet won't take long with the right technology.	☐	☐

Will in Statements		
Subject	***Will* + Base Verb**	
I He They	will live won't live	on Mars one day.

Notes:
- Use *will* to predict a future event. Example: *We will live on Mars.*
- Use *will* for a promise. Example: *I will write to you every day.*
- Use *will* when making decisions at the time of speaking.
- *Be going to* and *will* predict the future. Use *be going to* or present progressive for plans.

Will in Yes/No Questions

Will	Subject	Base Verb		Short Answer	
Will	we she people	live	on Mars one day?	Yes, we will. Yes, she will. Yes, they will.	No, we won't. No, she won't. No, they won't.

Information Questions with Will

Wh- Word/How Phrase	Will	Subject	Base Verb	
When	will	humans	terraform	other planets?
How long	will	it	take	to terraform a planet?

C Complete the report using *will* and the verbs in the box.

not be   search   turn   cost   take   dig   plant   create   send   move   solve   ~~not be~~

Special Report on Terraforming Mars

1.1 Procedure

How will scientists and engineers terraform Mars? It ___won't be___ (1) easy. First,

engineers _____ (2) an atmosphere on Mars. They _____ (3) special robots

to Mars. These robots _____ (4) the planet's surface to find water.

The robots _____ (5) very deep into the core. Then, they _____ (6) seeds

and grow the plants to make oxygen. The plants _____ (7) carbon dioxide in the

Martian atmosphere and _____ (8) it into oxygen. After many years, animals and

people _____ (9) to Mars.

1.2 Advantages

Terraforming _____ (10) problems of pollution, lack of resources, and

overpopulation on Earth.

1.3 Disadvantages

Terraforming Mars _____ (11) cheap. It _____ (12) billions of dollars.

D Listen to this interview with a scientist. Write the questions using *will*.

Interviewer: _____

Dr. Sarru: Yes, I think we will live on other planets.

Interviewer: _____

Dr. Sarru: Not for a long time. I don't think people will live on Mars

        anytime soon.

Interviewer: _____

Dr. Sarru: I think some people will want to live on Mars.

Interviewer: _____

Dr. Sarru: I think so. Many people will want to stay on Earth.

Interviewer: _____

Dr. Sarru: Yes, they will. Astronauts will fly to Mars soon.

Interviewer: _____

Dr Sarru: I'm not sure what we'll call people on Mars. Martians, I suppose.

E The people below are characters in a science fiction story. Imagine you are the main character and the characters here are friends of yours. Look at the situations. Think of some things you will buy or do for them. Use *will* or *won't*.

1. Peter is moving to Mars.

    _____ *I'll have a going-away party for him.* _____

2. Jerzy is visiting Mars. He hates flying.

    _____

3. Henri misses food from Earth.

    _____

4. Julie says it's too hot on Mars.

    _____

5. Suzi is on Mars. She misses you very much.

    _____

F Look at the picture. Write sentences with the promises the pilot is making. Use *will* and the words in parentheses.

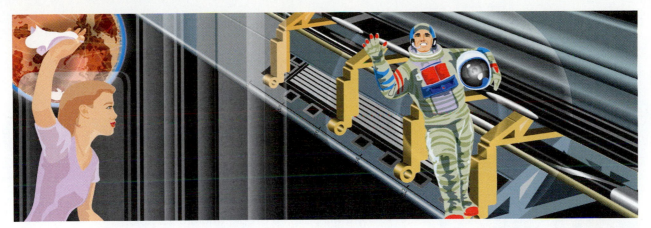

1. (write every day) _____ *I'll write every day.* _____

2. (love, always) _____

3. (fly safely) _____

4. (be home soon) _____

5. (not eat too much Martian food) _____

6. (not look at Martian women) _____

■ **C O M M U N I C A T E**

G **PAIR WORK** Work with a classmate. Make two predictions about your future. Use *will* and *won't.*

In 5 years...   In 10 years...   In 30 years...   In 50 years...

H **WRITE** Write a paragraph about what you found out in exercise G.

■ G R A M M A R   I N   C O N T E N T

A **Read and listen.**

CD2,TR22

What Will Earth Be Like in 2099?

Isaac Asimov was a science fiction writer. He wrote many books about the future of Earth. Some people think the ideas from his stories will come true. Here are some of Asimov's predictions:

- **There will be** equality between men and women.
- **There will be** more people who are very old.
- **There will be** new medicines. These medicines will mean people won't get sick.
- **There won't be** any wars.
- **There will be** one government for all countries.
- **There will be** more exploration of space.
- **There will be** factories in space. This means there will be less pollution on Earth.

equality: a condition of being equal

B **Check (✔) *True* or *False*.**

	True	False
1. Asimov said that people will live longer.	☐	☐
2. He mentioned that there will be more racism.	☐	☐
3. He expected that there will be more factories in space.	☐	☐
4. He predicted that there will be more wars on Earth.	☐	☐

There + *Will* Statements		
There	*Will be*	Subject
There	will be	peace.
There	won't be	

Notes:

- *There + will/won't be* says that something will or won't exist.
- Use expressions of time. Examples: *in 50 years, in the future.*

C Use the lecture notes below to write about what some writers think will happen to Earth. Use *there + be going to* or *will be*.

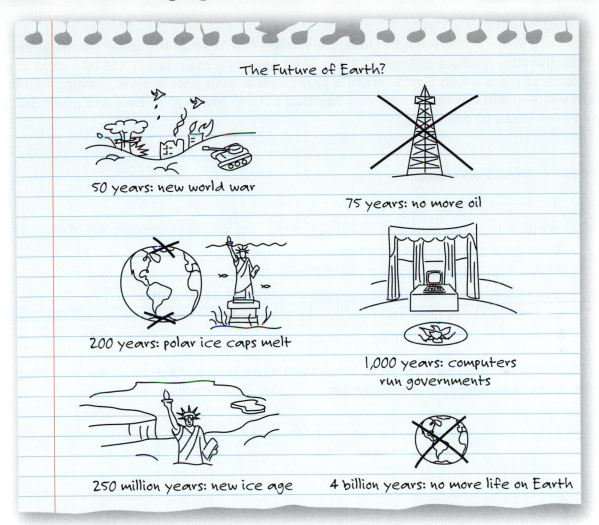

The Future of Earth?

50 years: new world war

75 years: no more oil

200 years: polar ice caps melt

1,000 years: computers run governments

250 million years: new ice age

4 billion years: no more life on Earth

1. In 50 years, there will be _____.

2. In 75 years, _____.

3. In 200 years, _____.

4. _____.

5. _____.

6. _____.

■ COMMUNICATE

D GROUP WORK Discuss the predictions in exercise C and in the reading on page 186. Which of these things do you think will happen?

GRAMMAR AND VOCABULARY Imagine you are the head of the government agency that is planning a future colony on Mars. Your agency's main job is not to repeat the mistakes of the past on Earth. Write a paragraph in your notebook explaining what there will and will not be in your new Martian colony. Make promises and predictions. Read your ideas to the class.

PROJECT Report on change.

1. Work with two or three classmates.
2. What are your countries doing to change the world? Compare your answers with your classmates' answers.
3. Make a list of similarities and differences.
4. Discuss whether all of these changes are good or bad, and why.
5. Prepare a short presentation for the whole class.

 INTERNET Go online. Use the Web to find out more information about terraforming Mars. Share any interesting information with your classmates.

PART 1
Possibility: *May, Might, Could*

PART 2
Future Conditional with
Will, May, Might

Lesson (25)

Criminology: Forensics

■ CONTENT VOCABULARY

Look at the pictures. Do you know the words?

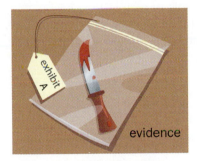

evidence

poison

a suspect

a witness

a detective

a crime scene

Write the new words in your vocabulary journal.

■ THINK ABOUT IT

If there is a crime, what do the police use to find the suspects? Discuss the question with your class.

189

■ **GRAMMAR IN CONTENT**

CD2,TR23

A **Read and listen.**

Forensic Science

Student: What do forensic scientists do?

Instructor: Forensic scientists find and interpret evidence at
             crime scenes. Imagine a person is dead and the
             police don't see a wound. Was it murder? What
             killed this person? It **may be** poison. It **could be** a
             drug. It **might not be** any of those things. It **may be**
             natural causes.

Student: What if it's murder?

Instructor: If it's murder, who killed this person? Crime scene
             investigators **may find** the murderer's hair or blood
             or a little piece of clothing. If it was poison, they
             might see something during the autopsy. Forensic
             scientists will find out.

---

to interpret: to translate from one language to another

to investigate: to look at something carefully, examine

an autopsy: a medical examination of a dead body

B **Check (✔)** *True* **or** *False.*

	True	False
1. A forensic scientist is a police officer.	☐	☐
2. A forensic scientist is a kind of detective.	☐	☐
3. Forensic scientists must be good in chemistry, math, biology, etc.	☐	☐
4. When forensic scientists know the cause of death, they perform an autopsy.	☐	☐

May, Might, and *Could* in Statements		
Subject	***May / Might / Could***	**Base Verb**
A forensic scientist	may might could ——— might not may not	find all the evidence.

Notes:

- *May, might,* and *could* mean that something is possible now or in the future.
- **Could not** means something is impossible. Example: *Henry was with me during the robbery. He* **couldn't be** *the robber!* (It's impossible that he is the robber.)
- Use *will* or *be going to* when you are more certain about the future. Example: *I'm* **going to find** *the criminal.*
- *Maybe* is sometimes used with *will.* Example: *Maybe a forensic scientist* **will find** *the evidence.* (NOT: ~~Maybe a forensic scientist may find the evidence.~~)

C Complete the conversations with *may, may not, might, might not, could, could not,* and the verbs in the box.

| lead | not be | ~~leave~~ | be | have | kill |

1. **A:** Is his passport missing?

   B: Yes.

   A: Hmmm. It means he _____may leave_____ the country.

2. **A:** Look! There's a bag over there.

   B: Be careful! It _____ explosives in it.

3. **A:** Are there fingerprints on the knife?

   B: Yes, there are.

   A: They _____ the murderer's.

4. **A:** Should we take him to the police station?

   B: No. Let's follow him. He _____ us to the stolen jewels.

5. **A:** She must be the murderer!

   B: No. She was in a different city. She _____ the murderer.

6. **A:** If the police don't stop her, do you think she will kill again?

   B: I'm not sure. She _____ again.

D Imagine you are a forensic scientist. There was a robbery last night in an apartment. Someone was hurt. Look at the pictures below. Write sentences using *may, might,* and *could.*

1. The neighbor _____.

2. Suzi _____.

3. The knife _____.

4. The doorknob _____.

5. The hair _____.

E Read about Jill. (Circle) the correct words to complete the sentences. Sometimes, more than one choice is correct.

Jill is a forensic scientist. She is (going to investigate / may investigate) a murder downtown. She doesn't know all the
(1)
details. She thinks it (might be / will be) in the same building
(2)
as the murder last week. She's not sure how many other
forensic scientists (may work / will work) on this case. She (will be / could be) the
(3)   (4)
only one. When she arrives at the crime scene, she (will call / may call) her boss.
(5)
He (will tell / might tell) her to start the investigation, or he (may tell / will tell)
(6)   (7)
her to wait for help.

F **PAIR WORK** Work with a classmate. One of you should create a *Yes/No* question and an information question for pictures 1–3 in exercise D. The other person should do the same for pictures 4–6. Use *could* in your *Yes/No* questions. Use *may, might,* or *could* in your information questions. Take turns asking each other questions and giving short answers and long answers.

Who might that figure in chalk be?

It might be the victim.

| PART TWO | Future Conditional with *Will, May, Might* |

■ GRAMMAR IN CONTENT

CD2,TR24

A Read the following passage about what happens to evidence that investigators find at a crime scene.

Handling the Evidence

When forensic scientists find evidence at a crime scene, they must be very careful with it. For example, **if they find** a gun, **they will pick** it **up** with something that doesn't put their fingerprints on it. **If they see** skin under the victim's fingernails, **they will put** small plastic bags over the victim's hand to protect this evidence.

Crime scene investigators are very careful not to touch the evidence. **They could contaminate** the evidence **if they touch** it with their bare hands. So they always wear special gloves. All the evidence goes into plastic bags if possible. **The police may have** a better case in court **if the forensic scientists keep** all the evidence uncontaminated.

to protect: to defend against harm or loss

to contaminate: to make unclean

a case: a good cause or reason for an action

B Check (✔) *True* or *False.*

	True	False
1. Police don't stop people visiting a crime scene.	☐	☐
2. Skin under a victim's fingernails could be the murderer's.	☐	☐
3. Investigators touch some pieces of evidence without gloves.	☐	☐
4. The evidence is put into the police car exactly as it is.	☐	☐

Future Conditional with *Will, May, Might*

If- + Simple Present	Secondary Clause
If he **finds** evidence,	it **may help** the police to solve a crime.
If they **don't have** strong evidence,	the police **might not arrest** anybody.
If she **is** innocent,	she **will go** free.
	she **won't go to** jail.

Notes:

- Use the future conditional to make predictions about what will happen in a situation. Example: *If she is innocent, she will go free.* (We don't know if she is innocent. It is a future event.)

- In the secondary clause, *will* means the future. It also means that the speaker or writer is sure about the future event. Compare the following two sentences:

  If they find evidence, it **may** help to solve a crime. (possible)

  If they find evidence, it **will** help to solve the crime. (sure)

- The verb in the *if-* clause never uses *will*. NOT: ~~If she will be innocent, she will go free.~~

- You can begin your statement with the secondary clause. When you do that, you don't use the comma. Example: *She will go free if she is innocent.*

C Read the dialogue between Lena, a forensic scientist, and the police chief. They are talking about a case. (Circle) the correct verb.

Chief: Do you think his wife Vivian killed him?

Lena: We don't know. If we (will find / find) poison in his body, we
(1)
(will have / have) a better idea.
(2)

Chief: But why did Vivian try to kill him?

Lena: Her husband was very rich. If he (will die / dies), she (may get / gets)
(3)   (4)
his whole fortune, $200 million!

Chief: Hmm. What does the autopsy report say?

Lena: The report isn't ready. We ('ll arrest / arrest) her if the report
(5)
(will show / shows) that it was poison.
(6)

Chief: What will you do if the report doesn't say that?

Lena: If it (doesn't say / won't say) that, we (won't have / don't have) any
(7)   (8)
other suspects—and Vivian Helms will be a very rich widow!

D Use the two groups of words to make a future conditional sentence. Use *will*, *may*, *might*, or *could* in your sentences.

1. police find a gun / have fingerprints

   If the police find a gun, it may have fingerprints on it.

2. she sees a crime / the police ask her questions

   _____

3. find blood at a crime scene / be the suspect's

   _____

4. a suspect is arrested / go to court

   _____

5. jury find her guilty of murder / she go to prison for life

   _____

E Look at these pictures. Write a sentence describing what you think will happen in the pictures. Use *If* and *will*, *may*, *might*, or *could*.

1. _If her husband doesn't see what she's doing, she will put the poison in his drink._

2. _____

3. _____

4. _____

F **PAIR WORK** Work with a classmate. What may/might/could happen in the following situations?

If the police lose evidence . . .

a criminal may go free.

1. If you steal from someone . . .
2. If you drive too fast . . .
3. If you see a crime . . .
4. If a criminal leaves fingerprints . . .

Connection | Putting It Together

GRAMMAR AND VOCABULARY Imagine that you are Superman or Wonder Woman. You have wonderful powers that normal people don't have. Think of ways you might use your powers to help investigate and solve crimes and also prevent crimes from happening. Write a paragraph. Use the grammar and vocabulary from the lesson.

PROJECT Discuss crime and punishment.

1. Work with one or two classmates.
2. Create a list of crimes. Write a punishment for each crime.
3. Exchange your list with another group's list.
4. Look over the other group's list and make changes to some of their punishments if you don't agree with them.
5. Discuss the changes that you want to make with the people in your group. Create conditional sentences to explain the reasons for your changes.
6. Present your list of crimes and punishments to the class and tell them the reasons for your changes to the original list.

The original list only gives six months in jail for not paying federal taxes. We don't think that's enough time. It should be six years, not six months. If a person gets only six months for this crime, he or she may do it again.

 INTERNET Go online. Search on the Web for forensic science. Find out the many different areas that professionals in forensics work in. Make a list of those areas. Talk to the class about what you found out.

A Complete this conversation between the convention manager of a large resort hotel and a possible customer for this service. Use the words in parentheses. Think of words to put in the other blanks.

Customer: Good morning. _____ I speak to your convention manager?
<u>(1)</u>

Clerk: Certainly, sir. _____ you wait here one moment, I (tell) _____ the
<u>(2)</u>   <u>(3)</u>

convention manager.

Manager: Good morning, sir. How _____ I help you?
<u>(4)</u>

Customer: I'm from the American Association of Forensic Scientists. We (have)

_____ our annual convention in this city next year. I (like)
<u>(5)</u>

_____ to know _____ your hotel _____ large enough for
<u>(6)</u>   <u>(7)</u>   <u>(8)</u>

our needs.

Manager: How many people _____ there _____?
<u>(9)</u>   <u>(10)</u>

Customer: There _____ 5,000 members for sure, but we (have) _____ as
<u>(11)</u>   <u>(12)</u>

many as 8,000.

Manager: That's fine. Even _____ you (have) _____ 8,000 members at
<u>(13)</u>   <u>(14)</u>

the convention, we (have) _____ enough rooms for everyone.
<u>(15)</u>

Customer: _____ an organization (bring) _____ 8,000 people to your
<u>(16)</u>   <u>(17)</u>

hotel, _____ you offer a discount on the hotel rooms?
<u>(18)</u>

Manager: Yes, we _____. _____ 5,000 members (reserve) _____
<u>(19)</u>   <u>(20)</u>   <u>(21)</u>

rooms, we (offer) _____ a 6% discount on rooms. If _____ 8,000
<u>(22)</u>   <u>(23)</u>

members or more, we (give) _____ a 10% discount.
<u>(24)</u>

Customer: That's very good.

B Wafa is interviewing for an LPN position in a small hospital. Complete this part of the conversation between her and Ms. Klein, the head of nursing. Use the words in parentheses. Think of words to put in the other blanks.

Wafa: _____(1) you repeat that, please?

Ms. Klein: Sure. _____(2) you get this position, _____(3) you stay with the hospital for a long time or leave after just one or two years?

Wafa: I (like) _____(4) to keep this job for many years. I (look) _____(5) for another job _____(6) I'm happy working in this hospital. Why _____(7) you ask that question?

Ms. Klein: I _____(8) completely honest with you. Many LPNs come and go. They get good experience here, and then they look for larger hospitals or they move.

Wafa: That's not me, Ms. Klein. I (want) _____(9) to work in a small hospital. I (like) _____(10) to make a difference, and a small hospital (give) _____(11) me that chance. _____(12) I get this position, I promise that I (quit) _____(13) to work in a larger hospital.

Ms. Klein: _____(14) very glad to hear that.

LEARNER LOG Check (✔) *Yes* or *I Need More Practice.*

Lesson	I Can Use . . .	Yes	I Need More Practice
21	*Can* and *May* for Permission, *Can, Could,* and *Would* for Requests, and *Want* vs. *Would Like* for Desires		
22	Factual Conditional Statements and Questions		
23	*Be Going To* and the Present Progressive for Future Actions		
24	*Will* for Future Predictions, Promises, Certainty, and the Expression *There Will Be*		
25	*May, Might,* and *Could* for Possibility and the Future Conditional with *Will, May, Might*		

PART 1
The Zero Article with
Geographical Features

PART 2
The Definite Article with
Geographical Features

Lesson 26

Business: Tourism

■ CONTENT VOCABULARY

Look at the pictures. Do you know the words?

a mountain range

a canal

a canyon

a harbor

an island

Write the new words in your vocabulary journal.

■ THINK ABOUT IT

Are there special places to visit where you live? What are they? Why are they special and popular? Discuss these questions with your classmates.

■ **G R A M M A R   I N   C O N T E N T**

CD2,TR25

A Read and listen to this conversation between Craig, a travel agent, and Daniel and Emma, a young engaged couple in New York City.

Destination: Honeymoon

Daniel: We're planning our honeymoon. We like to drive, so we want to take a car trip. First we'll visit relatives in **Spring Valley.** Can you suggest other places to go from there?

Craig: I certainly can. After you see your relatives, drive up to **Lake Placid.** Stop in towns along the way. The area is just beautiful. Visit **Whiteface Mountain** and the great hotel at the top with its romantic views. Not far away is **Letchworth State Park.** The wildlife and scenery in the park are amazing.

Emma: That sounds great.

Craig: OK, I'll create a plan for you, and make the reservations.

---

scenery: nature, such as trees, mountains, sky, etc.

B Check (✔) *True* or *False.*

	True	False
1. Daniel and Emma are planning their honeymoon.	☐	☐
2. They are going to fly to Lake Placid.	☐	☐
3. It's too late to make reservations.	☐	☐

The Zero Article with Geographical Features		
	Zero Article	**Geographical Feature**
I'm going to	Ø	Mount Everest. Lake Geneva. Bolivia. Easter Island.

Note:

Don't use an article with:

1. names of lakes, individual mountains, and bays
2. names of continents, most countries, states, and cities
3. names of most islands

C Read each conversation. If you think it is correct to use the zero article and not the definite article (*the*), put a line through the definite article.

1. **A:** Where is the Taj Mahal?
   B: In ~~the~~ India.
2. **A:** What's the Yellowstone Park?
   B: It's a huge national park in the West. It's in the Wyoming, Montana, and Idaho.
3. **A:** You went to the United Kingdom last summer. Did you see the Sherwood Forest?
   B: Yes, we did. We traveled all over the England, Scotland, and Wales.
4. **A:** We're buying a summer home in the Oregon right in the mountains.
   B: It's beautiful there! I think that the Mt. Rainier and the Mt. Shasta are magnificent.
5. **A:** I understand that the Lake Erie has lots of pollution. Is that true?
   B: Yes, it is. Actually, all the Great Lakes are very polluted now.
6. **A:** Where are you going on vacation next summer?
   B: To the Whidbey Island, where a friend of mine lives. It's in the Pacific Northwest.
7. **A:** What about you? Are you going anywhere on vacation next summer?
   B: No, we're going in the winter, to the Eleuthra Island in the Bahamas.

■ COMMUNICATE

D **PAIR WORK** Fill out the form below. Share this information with a classmate. Take turns telling each other about your countries.

Country _____

Continent _____

Major cities _____

Famous places (lakes, parks, tourist areas) _____

_____

_____

_____

_____

_____

_____

■ GRAMMAR IN CONTENT

A Read and listen.

CD2,TR26

Touring South America

A tour company needs to do many things to arrange a tour or a cruise. It books airlines and ships. It reserves hotel rooms. It hires tour guides.

Craig recently planned a tour in South America for a senior citizens' group. His plan was for them to visit **the Andes Mountains** in Peru. He also planned a visit to **the Altiplano,** an amazing flat area in **the highlands** of Bolivia. The tour also included a cruise down **the Amazon River** and a good look at **the Amazon Rain Forest.**

to book: to save (reserve) a seat or room   **to hire:** to give someone a job
senior citizen: a polite term for someone over 65 years old

B Check (✔) *True* or *False.*

	True	False
1. Tour companies only book airlines and hotels.	☐	☐
2. Craig arranged a tour in South Africa.	☐	☐
3. The tour included a cruise down the Amazon River.	☐	☐

The Definite Article with Geographical Features

	the	Geographical Feature
I'm going to	**the**	Bahamas.
		Grand Canyon.
		Andes.
		Great Wall of China.
		Dominican Republic.

Notes:

• Use the definite article before the names of the following geographical features: rivers, oceans, gulfs, canyons, mountain ranges, and deserts.

• Use the definite article with natural and man-made regions (*the Arctic, the Middle East, the Hague*).

• For geographical features with many parts, make the name plural and don't mention the feature (*the Bahamas, the Himalayas*).

• Some countries include the definite article (*the United States of America*).

C Read the e-mail from Dale, the owner of a tour company. Circle the definite or zero article to complete the sentences.

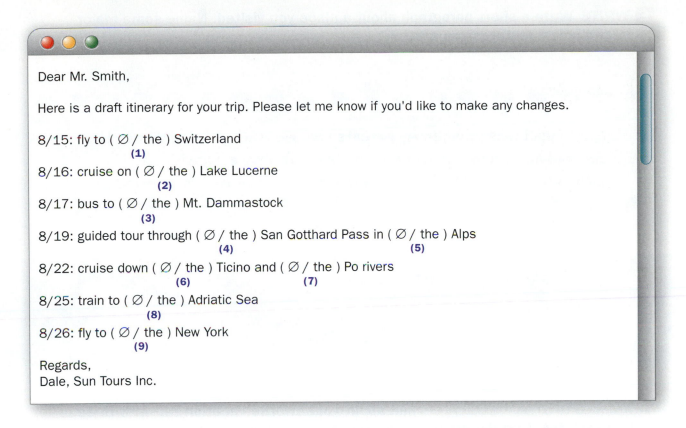

Dear Mr. Smith,

Here is a draft itinerary for your trip. Please let me know if you'd like to make any changes.

8/15: fly to (∅ / the) Switzerland
           (1)

8/16: cruise on (∅ / the) Lake Lucerne
              (2)

8/17: bus to (∅ / the) Mt. Dammastock
           (3)

8/19: guided tour through (∅ / the) San Gotthard Pass in (∅ / the) Alps
                        (4)   **(5)**

8/22: cruise down (∅ / the) Ticino and (∅ / the) Po rivers
                (6)   **(7)**

8/25: train to (∅ / the) Adriatic Sea
             (8)

8/26: fly to (∅ / the) New York
           (9)

Regards,
Dale, Sun Tours Inc.

D Read this conversation between Dale, the owner of a tour company, and one of his best agents, Bree. For the blanks, decide if you need to add the word *the* or if you should keep the zero article.

Dale: Can you tell me about the tour you are planning?

Bree: Sure. I booked a flight for the group to _____ San Francisco,
                                                              (1)

_____ California. First, they will visit _____ Monterey Peninsula.
  (2)   **(3)**

Then they will travel north to _____ Sonoma County and take
                                  (4)

kayaks on _____ Russian River. After that, they'll travel east to
             (5)

see _____ Sacramento, _____ capital of _____ California.
      (6)   **(7)**   **(8)**

Next, they'll spend a couple of days at _____ Lake Tahoe. We'll fly
                                           (9)

to _____ Oregon after that to visit _____ Crater Lake National
     (10)   **(11)**

Park, and go on to _____ Portland, _____ City of _____ Roses.
                      (12)   **(13)**   **(14)**

Our tour will end in _____ Washington state.
                        (15)

Dale: Well, that sounds wonderful, Bree.

E WRITE Write a short paragraph about a place you visited. Name some major geographical features you saw.

> When I was younger, my parents took me during the winter to the Adirondacks, a mountain range in New York State. We visited Adirondack State Park. We saw Avalanche Lake and Mt. Marcy.

Connection   Putting It Together

GRAMMAR AND VOCABULARY Talk about your favorite vacation trip with three or four classmates. Use the grammar and vocabulary in this lesson.

PROJECT Work together with two of your classmates. Write a skit (a short scene) about a tour company. Each person in your group should have a role.

1. Decide who the tour agent is. The two other people want to plan a tour.
2. Choose an itinerary for the tour.
3. Do a search on the Internet or look through a world atlas to find places that will make this tour interesting.
4. Write the skit. Ask your teacher to check your work.
5. Rehearse (practice) your skit and perform it for the whole class.

  INTERNET Go online. Find a geographical feature for each name below. In your notebook, write down what kind of feature each one is.

1. Canaveral	5. Baikal	9. Penrhyn	13. Biggin
2. Etna	6. Chirombo	10. Batemans	14. Clova
3. Hobe	7. Everglades	11. Napa	15. Daytona
4. Perdido Key	8. Bondi	12. Staten	16. Wachusett

Performing Arts: In the Theater

■ CONTENT VOCABULARY

Look at the pictures. Do you know the words?

a show/musical

a theatrical production

a spotlight

a spotlight operator

a carpenter

a play

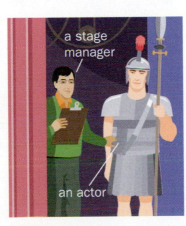

a stage manager

an actor

a theater/stage

a sound technician

to learn lines

a rehearsal

Write the new words in your vocabulary journal.

■ THINK ABOUT IT

Have you ever been to the theater? When was the last time you went? Why do people go to the theater? Discuss these questions with your classmates.

■ **GRAMMAR IN CONTENT**

CD2,TR27

A Read and listen.

Andrew Lloyd Webber

Andrew Lloyd Webber is a composer. He was born in London in 1948. He started writing musicals in 1965. His musicals **have been** very popular **for** over 30 years. All of his musicals **have not been** hits, but most **have been**. He wrote the musical *Phantom of the Opera*. It **has been** a popular musical on Broadway **since** 1980.

composer: someone who writes music

a hit: a great success

B Check (✔) *True* or *False*.

	True	False
1. Andrew Lloyd Webber was born in the middle of the nineteenth century.	☐	☐
2. All of his shows have been hits.	☐	☐
3. *Phantom of the Opera* is not popular.	☐	☐

The Present Perfect: Affirmative Statements with *For* and *Since*

Subject	*Have*	Been Participle		*For* or *Since*
I You We They	have have not haven't	been	married	**for** a long time. **for** six months. **for** five minutes.
She He	has hasn't			**since** 1995. **since** last year.

Notes:

• Use the present perfect to show that an action began in the past and continues into the present. Example: *Peter **has been** at the Shubert Theater since 1986.* (He started there in 1986. He still works there now.)

• Use *for* when talking about a length of time (a century, a decade, a week, a long time, 25 years, a while, etc.).

• Use *since* when talking about a specific time or event when something began (1995, the 20th century, the party, high school).

• Use the contractions (*I've, you've, he's, she's, it's, we've, they've*) in conversational English. We don't usually use the contractions in formal speaking or writing.

C Complete the sentences with the present perfect of *be* and *for* or *since.*

1. Griselda writes plays. She _____ a playwright _____ over 25 years.

2. Gavin is acting right now. He _____ on stage _____ 20 minutes. He _____ an actor _____ two years.

3. Bernard and Karen became sound technicians only last year. They _____ sound technicians _____ a long time.

4. Donna is a stage manager. She is a member of the Actors' Equity Association. She _____ a member _____ over five years.

5. Max is a spotlight operator. He _____ a spotlight operator _____ high school.

6. Ricardo was a theatrical carpenter for many years. He _____ in a theater _____ he retired.

7. Ryan is a singer and dancer. He _____ in musicals _____ he arrived in New York from Boise, Idaho. He _____ a singer _____ eight years.

8. Julie and Millie want to be singers, but they aren't working. They _____ employed _____ last fall.

■ **COMMUNICATE**

D **WRITE** Write a paragraph about yourself or someone you know well. Use the present perfect of *be* and *for* and *since.*

My name is Tomek. I live in Miami. I have been in Miami for two years. My wife's name is Susan. We have been married for six months. I am friends with Ella. She has been in Miami since she was a little girl.

■ GRAMMAR IN CONTENT

CD2,TR28

A Read and listen.

On Broadway

Broadway is a long street in New York City. It has some of the best theaters in the world. Broadway theaters **have entertained** millions of people **for** a very long time.

The first great theater on Broadway was the Daly Theater. It opened in 1869. **Since** then, more than 70 theaters **have opened** on or near Broadway. The newest theater is called the Ford Center. It **has had many** great plays and shows **since** 1997.

For more than a century, success on Broadway **has meant** success all over the country—and often all over the world.

success: a great event, achievement

entertain: to amuse

B Check (✔) *True* or *False*.

	True	False
1. Broadway has been the home of great theater since the mid-1800s.	☐	☐
2. There are 70 theaters on Broadway now.	☐	☐
3. The Ford Center has offered plays and shows since 1869.	☐	☐
4. People all around the world have heard of Broadway.	☐	☐

Some Past Participles					
Basic Verb	**Simple Past**	**Past Participle**	**Basic Verb**	**Simple Past**	**Past Participle**
be	was, were	**been**	sing	sang	**sung**
have	had	**had**	teach	taught	**taught**
know	knew	**known**	think	thought	**thought**
learn	learned	**learned**	want	wanted	**wanted**
live	lived	**lived**	write	wrote	**written**
see	saw	**seen**	work	worked	**worked**

C Complete each sentence using the words in parentheses and the present perfect with *for* and *since*.

1. (He / work / three theaters / 2001)

   Nelson is an artistic director. _He has worked in three theaters since 2001._

2. (They / know / each other / 5 years)

   Bob and Cheryl are actors. _____

3. (He / have / this job / last July)

   Philippe is a make-up artist. _____

4. (She / learn / half of her lines / this morning)

   Keisha is learning her part in the play. _____

5. (They / not practice / many weeks)

   The dancers are rehearsing. _____

6. (She / teach / dancers / 25 years)

   Erica is a dance instructor. _____

7. (2 hours / Suzy /watch / rehearsals)

   Suzy is a casting director. _____

8. (He / not see / many plays / recently)

   Ahmed likes the theater. _____

D Correct these paragraphs. There are five more errors.

Mark and Jenna are actors who are married to each other. They have been married ~~since~~ ^for^ 23 years. They live and work in Toronto. They have lived there for 1993. They have been actors since many years. Since they got married, Mark and Jenna worked in three plays together.

At the moment they are at a rehearsal for a new play. They have rehearse every day for the past six weeks. They are having a difficult time because the playwright changed many lines since rehearsals began.

E **GROUP WORK** Work in groups of three and take turns. The first student secretly tells the second student something using the present perfect. The second student secretly repeats the information to the third student of the group. The third student reports back to the first student, saying what he/she thinks the first student said.

My brother hasn't seen a musical.

Ahmad's brother hasn't seen a musical.

José says your brother hasn't seen a musical.

Connection | Putting It Together

GRAMMAR AND VOCABULARY Write a paragraph in your notebook about one person (yourself or somebody you know very well). Write about some things that the person has done or hasn't done, and use *for* and *since.* Read your paragraph to the class.

My cousin Muzyad has played the acoustic guitar and written songs since he was in middle school. He has worked in a rock band for a few years. Unfortunately, his band has not had any big hits.

 INTERNET PROJECT Go online and prepare a presentation for your class. Search for information about theaters on Broadway or in a city you like. Find out the following:

- the history of the theater
- what shows have played there
- what actors have acted there

Performing Arts: Film Studies

▪ CONTENT VOCABULARY

Look at the pictures. Do you know the words?

a camera

a director

a studio

a star

a fan

a script

Star Searcher: The Movie

an audition

Write the new words in your vocabulary journal.

▪ THINK ABOUT IT

Have you seen any of these movies?

Terminator *Casablanca* *King Kong*

The Godfather *Gone with the Wind* *The Lord of the Rings*

Discuss your opinions of these or other movies with your classmates.

■ GRAMMAR IN CONTENT

A Read and listen.

CD2,TR29

> **Hollywood: Then and Now (Part One)**
>
> **Instructor:** Class, please welcome our guest, Hollywood movie star since the 1940s, Ms. Victoria Flame. Thank you for coming to talk to us about Hollywood, Ms. Flame. Do you have any questions for our famous guest?
>
> **Jill:** **Has** Hollywood **changed** since the 1940s, Ms. Flame?
>
> **Victoria:** **Yes, it has.** Many things have changed. In those days, the major studios controlled everything: actors, directors, even movie theaters. **Have you heard** of the studio system?
>
> **Jill:** **No, I haven't.**
>
> **Victoria:** Actors and directors had to sign contracts with just one studio. They couldn't work for anybody else. Many people in Hollywood were upset about this system. There was no freedom.
>
> **Lyle:** **Have** some things **stayed** the same in Hollywood since the '40s?
>
> **Victoria:** Yes, some things have. There has always been a star system. Fans love finding out about the lives of movie stars. The movie studios love it because people watch more movies.
>
> **Paolo:** **Have** you **made** any movies recently, Ms. Flame?
>
> **Victoria:** No, I haven't. I'm retired.
>
> **Kim:** **How long has** it **been** since your last movie?
>
> **Victoria:** My goodness! It's been many years since I made my last movie.

B Check (✔) *True* or *False*.

	True	False
1. Victoria Flame was a movie star.	☐	☐
2. The star system has disappeared from Hollywood.	☐	☐
3. Victoria is making movies today.	☐	☐

The Present Perfect: *Yes/No* Questions and Short Answers

Have	Subject	Past Participle		Short Answers
Have	you			Yes, I have.
				No, I haven't.
		seen	the movie?	
Has	she			Yes, she has.
				No, she hasn't.

The Present Perfect: *How Long*

How Long	Have	Subject			
	have	you I we they			
How long	————————		lived	here?
	has	she he it			

C Complete the conversation between a movie producer and a student. Use present perfect questions. Use *how long* where necessary.

Producer: I know you're a student at the community college.

_____ you
(1)

_____ (go) there?

Student: For about eight months.

Producer: _____ you _____ (be) in
(2)

the film arts program long?

Student: No, I _____. I enrolled in the program six
(3)

months ago.

Producer: _____ you _____ (want) to
(4)

be a screenwriter?

Student: Since I was a kid. I've always wanted to write for the movies.

_____ you _____ (read) the script
(5)

I sent you?

Producer: No, I _____. _____ you
(6)   (7)

_____ (written) a movie script?

Student: Yes, I _____. I hope you take a look at it.
(8)

D Use the answers to write present perfect questions.

1. **Q:** _How long have you been in the film arts program?_

   A: I've been in the program for five months.

2. **Q:** _____

   A: No, I haven't seen any old movies.

3. **Q:** _____

   A: They have wanted to be actors since they were kids.

4. **Q:** _____

   A: The movie's been on for about half an hour.

5. **Q:** _____

   A: No, I haven't heard of that movie.

6. **Q:** _____

   A: She's been a director for twenty years.

7. **Q:** _____

   A: Yes, many of her movies have been hits.

8. **Q:** _____

   A: Yes, Kim has taken a movie production class.

◼ COMMUNICATE

E **PAIR WORK** Work with a classmate. Imagine you are actors waiting to have an audition with a director for a new movie. Student A, use the resume on page 215. Student B, use the resume on page 237. Take turns asking about each other's experiences. Use the present perfect and simple past.

Student A

Movies
A Creeping Shadow (2005)
Murder Most Horrid (2004)

TV
Years of Our Lives (2002–present)
Children's Zoo (2000–2002)

Awards
Best Children's Performer, Kid TV Network (2001)

Education
City Film School – Film Studies Certificate (2006–present)
Drama School (1998–1999)

Student A Questions
1. be / in any movies?
2. be / in any TV shows?
3. How long / be / on *Laughs and Laughs*?
4. win / any awards?
5. be / to drama school?
6. How long / be / film school?

PART TWO	The Present Perfect: *Ever, Never*

■ **GRAMMAR IN CONTENT**

A **Read and listen.**

CD2, TR30

Hollywood: Then and Now (Part Two)

Instructor: Ms. Flame, have you **ever** worked with other famous movie stars?

Victoria: What a question! Of course I have, dear!

Jill: How about Tom Cruise? Have you **ever** been in a movie with him?

Victoria: No, I've **never** appeared with Tom Cruise.

Lyle: Well, have you **ever** made a movie with Madonna or Brad Pitt?

Victoria: Hmm . . . No, I have **never** had the honor of working with them either. But have you young people **ever** heard of Clark Gable or Montgomery Clift or Lana Turner? I worked with all of them.

Instructor: They've **never** heard of those movie stars. Sorry, Ms. Flame. I guess they're too young.

B Check (✔) *True* or *False*.

	True	False
1. Victoria Flame worked with many movie stars.	☐	☐
2. She has worked with Tom Cruise.	☐	☐
3. The students have heard of Montgomery Clift.	☐	☐

The Present Perfect: Questions with *Ever*

Have	Subject	*Ever*	Past Participle	
Have	you	**ever**	been	to Hollywood?

The Present Perfect: Answers to *Ever* Questions

Yes, I **have.**
Yes, I**'ve been** to Hollywood.
Yes, I went there last year.
_____

No, I **haven't.**
No, I**'ve never** been to Hollywood.

Notes:

• *Ever* means "at any time." For a person, that means from the time he/she was born to now.

• Always put *ever* between the subject and the past participle.

• For vague or general "yes" answers use the present perfect. Example: *Yes, I**'ve seen** that movie.*

• For "yes" answers about experiences or events, use the simple past. Example: *Yes, I **saw** that movie last year.*

C Use the words to write a present perfect question using *ever*. Then write answers about yourself for each question. Use the past simple if appropriate.

1. (you / ever / visit / Hollywood)

   Q: _____ Have you ever visited Hollywood? _____

   A: _____

2. (your best friend / ever / be / in a movie)

   Q: _____

   A: _____

3. (you / ever / meet / a movie star)

Q: _____

A: _____

4. (they / ever / see / a film in English)

Q: _____

A: _____

5. (you / ever / wanted to be in a movie)

Q: _____

A: _____

6. (your brother or sister / ever / go / to the movies on a date)

Q: _____

A: _____

■ **COMMUNICATE**

D **GROUP WORK** Work in small groups. Take turns asking and answering the questions below. Use the present perfect with *ever* and *never*.

Have you ever seen a Hollywood movie studio?

No, I haven't. I've never seen one.

1. buy popcorn / the movies?
2. see a Hollywood movie?
3. want / to be an actor?
4. want / to be a director?
5. be / in a movie?
6. left / a theater in the middle of a movie?

GRAMMAR AND VOCABULARY Interview some classmates. Find out who has done the following things and who has never done the following things. Take notes and tell the class what you have found out about those classmates.

- acted in a school play
- directed a show
- written a play or screenplay
- worked in a theater or movie house
- met a well known actor
- bought and read magazines about performers (actors, singers, etc.)

 INTERNET PROJECT Work with a classmate. Prepare a short report on an American movie star, or one from another country. Search on the Internet for information about him or her. Give a presentation for your class. Find out the following:

- when and where he/she was born
- how long ago his/her career started
- how long he/she has been a star
- famous movies he/she has been in
- current project, if there is one

For your presentation, one of you should ask the questions and the other person should give the answers.

Earth Science: Global Warming

■ CONTENT VOCABULARY

Look at the pictures. Do you know the words?

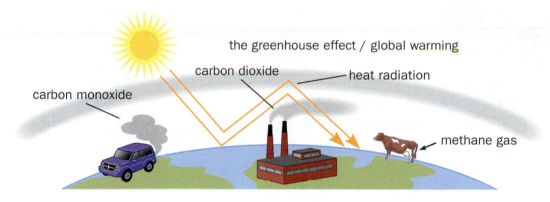

the greenhouse effect / global warming

carbon dioxide

heat radiation

carbon monoxide

methane gas

fossil fuels

a power station

Write the new words in your vocabulary journal.

■ THINK ABOUT IT

**Do you know about global warming? Do you know some of its possible effects?
Discuss these questions with your class.**

■ GRAMMAR IN CONTENT

A **Read and listen.**

CD2,TR31

Earth Day (Part I)

Nate: So Brenda, what's **the most important** issue on this year's Earth Day?

Brenda: That's **the easiest** question you can ask me. It's global warming, of course. Global warming is one of the **worst** problems at the moment. It's destroying our planet!

Nate: But global warming isn't a fact, is it? It's still just a theory.

Brenda: You think so? **The most famous** scientists in the world say it's real and that it's happening right now.

Nate: And what are **the greatest** causes of global warming?

Brenda: Carbon dioxide and methane, two of the "greenhouse gases." Greenhouse gases keep too much heat from the sun in Earth's atmosphere. They're **the most dangerous** cause of global warming.

Earth Day: a yearly international event for the health of the planet

an issue: a topic or matter of concern

a theory: an idea, argument that something is true

B **Check (✔) *True* or *False*.**

	True	False
1. Brenda knows more about global warming than Nate does.	☐	☐
2. Brenda and Nate agree about what is the most important issue right now.	☐	☐
3. Most famous scientists feel that global warming is not a real danger to the planet.	☐	☐

Superlative Adjectives

	Superlative	
Global warming is	**the greatest**	problem on Earth.

Notes:

- Use the superlative form to talk about the first or last among three or more people or things.
- For one-syllable adjectives, put **the** before the adjective and add **-est** or **-st** to it. Examples: *the hottest, the nicest*
- *For* two-syllable adjectives ending in *-y,* put **the** before the adjective. Change the *-y* to *-i* and add **-est.** Examples: *the funniest, the healthiest*
- For two or more syllables, put **the most** before the adjective. Examples: *the most pleasant, the most difficult*
- Use **one of the** before the superlative adjective and add a plural noun. Example: *Pollution is one of the biggest problems in the United States.*
- It's usual to add a prepositional phrase to the end of the superlative. Examples: *in the world, on Earth, at the moment*
- Use the following superlatives for these irregular adjectives:
  good – the best; bad – the worst; far – the farthest (the furthest)

C **Complete the sentences by changing the adjectives in parentheses into superlative forms.**

1. The 1990s were (warm) _____the warmest_____ decade since records began.

2. The Arctic ice wall is (thin) _____ it has ever been.

3. Carbon dioxide is (common) _____ gas that contributes to global warming.

4. Coal is (popular) _____ fossil fuel used in power stations.

5. If global warming continues, scientists say parts of Europe will be

   _____ (dry) on Earth.

D **Complete the sentences using *one of the* and the words in parentheses.**

1. Mexico City is (polluted city) _one of the most polluted cities_ in the world.

2. India has been (bad polluter) _____ in the world.

3. New Zealand has (good record) _____ in controlling pollution.

4. The United States is (big producer) _____ of greenhouse gases in the world.

5. Reducing pollution is (important thing) _____ governments can do.

E GROUP WORK Interview some classmates. Ask and answer the questions below.

What is the most serious problem for our planet today?

Global warming is the most serious problem.

1. What's one of the most polluted places you've visited?
2. Which country is most responsible for global warming?
3. What's the worst problem in the world right now?

PART TWO	Superlative Adverbs

■ **GRAMMAR IN CONTENT**

A Read and listen.

CD2, TR32

> **Earth Day (Part II)**
>
> **Nate:** Okay, so greenhouse gases keep too much heat in the atmosphere, right?
>
> **Brenda:** Right. The extra heat is melting glaciers more quickly than scientists thought, and all that water is going into the oceans. With all that extra water, sea levels will go up. This will affect Florida and Bangladesh **the most immediately** and **the most dramatically**. They'll be under water because they're so close to sea level right now.
>
> **Nate:** My Aunt Millie lives in Florida. You mean her house will be under water?
>
> **Brenda:** Maybe. Luckily, many countries are taking the problem seriously. The countries taking it **the most seriously** are the ones that signed the Kyoto Accords.

dramatic: making a big impression

the Kyoto Accords: an agreement signed by 180 countries in 1997 to lower the amount of greenhouse gases by 2012

B Check (✔) *True* or *False.*

	True	False
1. There is too much heat in Earth's atmosphere.	☐	☐
2. Because Earth is getting warmer, glaciers are melting.	☐	☐
3. People who live on the coast won't really have a problem.	☐	☐
4. Nate is worried about his aunt.	☐	☐

Superlative Adverbs

Regular Adverb	Superlative	Irregular Adverb	Superlative
quickly	the most quickly	badly	the worst
carefully	the most carefully	well	the best
fast	the fastest	far	the farthest (the furthest)
early	the earliest		

Notes:
- For most superlatives, put **the most** before an adverb.
- You can add **of all** after this superlative form. Example: *Some cars use gas inefficiently. SUVs use gas the most inefficiently of all.*

C Use the adjectives in the box to complete the following paragraphs. Change them into adverbs and use superlative phrases.

> serious   good   fast   ~~quick~~   easy   effective   efficient

1. We are using fossil fuels very quickly. We are using oil
   _____*the most quickly*_____ of all. Many parts of the world have oil
   resources. Oil companies find fossil fuels _____ in the
   Middle East.

2. Many countries are serious about global warming. Countries that signed the
   Kyoto Accords want to stop global warming _____ .
   There are many ways to stop global warming. We can stop global warming
   _____ if we produce less carbon dioxide.

3. Some new cars use a fuel called ethanol. Ethanol is made from crops such
   as sugarcane or corn. Ethanol fuel works well in cars, but gasoline works
   _____ . Ethanol cars go fast, but gasoline cars go
   _____ . Ethanol drives an engine efficiently, but
   gasoline drives an engine _____ .

D **PAIR WORK** Interview a classmate. Use the groups of words to ask each other questions. Change adjectives into superlative adverbs.

What do you work the hardest to do?

I work the hardest to remember English vocabulary.

1. who – cook – good – anybody in your family?
2. who – live – far – from you – all your relatives?
3. in your family – who – get up – early?
4. where – bad – vacation – you – ever – take?
5. which subject in school – make – you – work – hard?

Connection | Putting It Together

GRAMMAR AND VOCABULARY Imagine Student A is a politician. Student B is a member of an environmental group. Student B wants to stop global warming. Perform a role play using the grammar and vocabulary from the lesson.

 INTERNET PROJECT Prepare a presentation about Earth's problems.

1. Work with two or three classmates.
2. Choose one of these problems: overpopulation, illegal drugs, air pollution, AIDS, terrorism.
3. Use the Internet to find out:
   - What are the causes?
   - What are the effects?
   - What are people doing to solve the problem?
   - Do you think people are doing enough?
   - Do you think people will find a solution?
4. Prepare a presentation to teach the class about the problem. Use pictures, charts, etc. for your presentation.

English: The History of the English Language

■ CONTENT VOCABULARY

Look at the pictures. Do you know the words?

communicate

language

Write the new words in your vocabulary journal.

■ THINK ABOUT IT

Do you know anything about the history of your language? What new words have been added to your language in the past years? Discuss with the class.

■ GRAMMAR IN CONTENT

CD2,TR33

A Read and listen to the following conversation between Dr. Jones, a university English teacher, and Bill, one of his students.

History of the English Language

Bill: Dr. Jones, can you please tell me something about the history of English?

Dr. J: I'd be happy to, Bill. But before I **begin**, you **need** to understand that three major groups of people **have influenced** the language we **speak**. In the sixth century, Germanic people **invaded** England from Denmark and northern Germany. They **were looking** for a new place to live. We **call** their language Anglo-Saxon.

Bill: **Were** people **living** in England at that time?

Dr. J: Yes, the Celts, but the Germanic people **pushed out** the Celts. Today the ancestors of the Celts live in Ireland, Scotland, and Wales.

Bill: So, **does** English **come** from Anglo-Saxon?

Dr. J: Remember that *three* groups **have made** the English language. The Vikings **decided** to invade England in the ninth century. They **spoke** Norse. When the two groups **came** together, they **chose** to call themselves the Saxons, and while life **was changing** in England, Anglo-Saxon and Norse **mixed**. English **was** born from that mixture.

Bill: Okay, so you**'re saying** that English **has** its roots in Anglo-Saxon and Norse.

Dr. J: Yes, but I **said** there **were** *three* groups, Bill. In 1066 the Normans from France **fought** the Saxons and **took** control of England. Their language, Norman French, **had** a big influence on English. Now you **know** about the three groups.

Bill: Wow, so English **has continued** to change for almost 1,000 years?

Dr. J: Yes, it **has**—and it **is** still **changing**.

influence: the power to change or persuade others

B Check (✔) *True* or *False*.

	True	False
1. English is a mixture of three languages.	☐	☐
2. People who spoke Norse came from Germany.	☐	☐
3. English has continued to change since the 11th century.	☐	☐
4. English is changing today.	☐	☐

Verb Form	Use/Meaning	Examples
simple past	1. an action finished in the past 2. shorter of two actions in the past	Germanic people **invaded** England. When they **arrived**, the Celts were living there.
past progressive	1. longer of two actions in the past 2. an action in progress in the past	When they arrived, the Celts **were living** there. The Celts **were living** peaceful lives at that time.
simple present	1. a habit or state 2. the present for stative verbs	People **speak** English in the U.S. People all over the world **want** to learn English.
present progressive	an action in the present	We **are learning** a little about the history of the English language.
present perfect	action from the past to the present	People **have spoken** English in the U.S. and Canada since the 1600s.

C Use the words in parentheses to complete this conversation between Harald, a Viking farmer, and his wife Frida.

Harald: Frida, _____ you (see) _____ all the activity in town
(1)
this morning?

Frida: Yes, Harald, I _____. A lot of people (leave) _____
(2) (3)
with all their possessions. I (think) _____ they (go)
(4)
_____ on some ships.
(5)

Harald: Yes, that's right! Knut (tell) _____ me that many ships
(6)
(leave) _____ since last week. The people (go) _____ to England
(7) (8)
to start new farms and new lives.

Frida: _____ (neg.) people (live) _____ in England now?
(9)

Harald: Yes, the Celts, but they (go) _____ away. They (want) _____ to
(10) (11)
live with us Vikings. They (move) _____ to other places.
(12)

Frida: Harald, I (want) _____ to leave this farm for a very long time.
(13)
It's terrible here. We only (have) _____ enough food for the animals
(14)
or ourselves.

Harald: _____ you (tell) _____ me that we should go to England, too?
(15)

Frida: Yes, Harald. That's exactly what I (say) _____. Let's go to England!
(16)

D Below are the answers to some questions about the conversation in exercise C. Create the questions for these answers.

1. _What did Harald and Frida see in the town that morning?_

They saw many people leaving the town with all their possessions.

2. _____

On some ships.

3. _____

The people were going to England.

4. _____

They wanted to start new farms and lives there.

5. _____

The Celts.

6. _____

Because they didn't want to live with the Vikings.

7. _____

Because their farm wasn't producing enough food for them or their animals.

■ **COMMUNICATE**

E Write two short paragraphs using the notes below. Use the simple past and past progressive in the first one. Use the simple present, present progressive, and present perfect in the second one. Write about the following in each paragraph:

First Paragraph
- first impressions of the instructor

- new classmates

- original feelings about this class

- ability to learn the lessons

Second Paragraph
- impressions of the instructor since the first day

- friendships with classmates for all these weeks

- feelings about this class since the beginning

- ability to learn the lessons during the whole course

When I first saw my teacher, she was writing some instructions for the students on the board. She seemed to be a little nervous. That was all right because most of the students were nervous, too.

Now I have known my teacher for three months. She has taught us a lot of English. I speak English better today than I did three months ago. This week we're learning more about grammar and about the history of the English language.

F **PAIR WORK** Work with a classmate. Exchange notebooks and read each other's paragraphs for exercise E. Correct any errors you find. Compare how similar or different your ideas are. Discuss what you both wrote.

PART TWO	Review: From Present to Future

■ GRAMMAR IN CONTENT

A Read and listen to this conversation between two English instructors.

CD2,TR34

conference: a professional meeting, usually at a hotel

colleague: a person with whom one works

The Future of the English Language

Betty: Hi, Richard. I want to ask you something. I'm **attending** a two-day conference next month on the future of English. Would you like to come?

Richard: That sounds interesting. How much **will** it **cost**?

Betty: Just $50.00 for registration. I'm **staying** with a friend who lives near there. She has a big house. She says that she'll **let** a colleague of mine stay there, too, if I ask her.

Richard: What **are** they **going to discuss** at the conference?

Betty: Future changes in grammar, word meanings, and new vocabulary that **will come** from technology, e-mailing, and the Web.

Richard: What about World English? It's **going to be** an important form of English in the future.

Betty: You're right. They're **having** a discussion about that on the second day of the conference. They're **going to talk** about what World English is.

Richard: Isn't it a form of English that non-English-speaking people use to communicate with one another?

Betty: Yes, it is. So, **are** you **coming** with me to the conference?

Richard: Absolutely! I'm sure it'll **be** very interesting.

B Check (✔) *True* or *False*.

	True	False
1. Betty is going to a concert next month.	☐	☐
2. Richard is asking her if he can go with her.	☐	☐
3. The conference will last for two days.	☐	☐
4. Richard probably won't have to pay for a hotel.	☐	☐
5. They're going to discuss lots of future changes to English.	☐	☐

Verb Form	Use/Meaning	Examples
present progressive	• for future plans that have been decided	They're **publishing** a new dictionary next year.
be going to	• for set plans in the future • for predictions about the near future • when current evidence makes us expect something to happen	The publishers **are going to include** many new computer terms in the new dictionary. English **is going to continue** to change. More and more people **are going to speak** English.
will	• for predictions about the future • to make a promise	World English **will be** very important one day. I'll **help** you with your grammar this afternoon.

C Read each sentence. If there is a mistake, make the correction. If there is no mistake, do nothing.

1. Okay, have a good day. I~~'m seeing~~ you at the conference. *ll see*

2. A group of linguists and English teachers are meeting next month in Tampa, Florida.

3. International business and the Internet will make World English more important in the future.

4. I'll go to a lecture on changes in the English verb system tonight. Want to join me?

5. I know the lecturer. She's a great speaker. I promise that you aren't feeling bored.

6. The college is offering a course on World English next semester. I'm going to take it.

D Here are some parts of English that students think are problems. Make predictions about them for far in the future. Use *be going to* and *will*, affirmative or negative.

1. I, you, we, they go. He, she, it goes.

   <u>In two hundred years, people will stop putting the -s or -es on verbs in the</u>
   <u>simple present.</u>

2. Do you see her? What does she have? Where did she get it?

   _____

   _____

3. mountain, night, pick, psychology, country, Wednesday

   _____

   _____

4. Her birthday is Thursday, August 3. He speaks Tamil and he's a Hindu.

   _____

   _____

5. dough ("doe" like "so"), tough (like "cuff"), through (like "threw")

   _____

   _____

6. World War II (Two), Elizabeth II (the Second), Chapter 2 (Two)

   _____

   _____

■ C O M M U N I C A T E

E GROUP WORK Ask three classmates to make predictions about their future. Use these topics or others: *careers, homes, children, travel.* Fill in the chart with their information. Tell the class what you have found out.

Classmate	Statements
Rigoberto	I'm going to be a cardiologist.
	I won't practice medicine in the U.S.

GRAMMAR AND VOCABULARY In your notebook, write a one-page report about everything you have done since you got up this morning and what you think you are going to do for the rest of the day and tonight. Use as many verb forms that we reviewed in this lesson as you can.

 INTERNET PROJECT Prepare a report on your language.

1. Work with two or three classmates who speak your native language.
2. Go to the library or search on the Internet for information about your language.
3. Find out the following information:

    *   language "family" your language belongs to
    *   major stages or periods in its development
    *   past influences on your language
    *   examples of current vocabulary and/or grammar changes
    *   future trends

4. Present your findings to your class.

A **Complete this conversation between two tourists at an airport. Use the words in parentheses in the blanks. If you find blanks with nothing in parentheses, think of something to put there or put nothing if you think that is correct.**

Chris: Are you going to _____ Bahamas or to _____ Trinidad and Tobago?
(1) (2)

Kyoko: Neither one. I'm flying to St. Croix in _____ U.S. Virgin Islands.
(3)

(be/you/ever) _____ there?
(4)

Chris: No, _____. Actually, I (be/never) _____ to _____ Caribbean.
(5) (6) (7)

Until three years ago, the (far) _____ I ever traveled was to college.
(8)

But things (change) _____ a lot _____ that time.
(9) (10)

Kyoko: Oh! You must visit _____ Caribbean islands! I think that area is
(11)

(beautiful) _____ and (relaxing) _____ part of _____ world!
(12) (13) (14)

Chris: Sorry, but I have to disagree with you. _____ Polynesia in _____
(15) (16)

South Pacific Ocean is (lovely) _____ and (calm) _____ area that
(17) (18)

I (visit/ever) _____. For example, _____ Hawaiian Islands are
(19) (20)

gorgeous! And _____ Hawaiians are (nice) _____ and
(21) (22)

(kind) _____ people you will ever meet!
(23)

Kyoko: Maybe so. But I have to tell you that the people on the islands around

_____ Caribbean Sea are (friendly) _____ people I know.
(24) (25)

_____ Hawaii is a part of _____ United States, right?
(26) (27)

(it/be) _____ a state _____ a long time?
(28) (29)

Chris: No, it (be) _____ a state very long, only _____ 1959. And in the
(30) (31)

1960s, _____ Honolulu, the capital, was growing (fast) _____ of all
(32) (33)

American cities for a while. People love it there.

Kyoko: Since I (begin) _____ traveling as a tourist, I (visit) _____ many
(34) (35)

Caribbean islands, but now I want to understand why you like _____
(36)

Polynesian Islands so much. I promise I'll go there next year!

B Complete this conversation between two community college instructors. Use the words in parentheses in the blanks. If you find blanks with nothing in parentheses, think of something to put there or put nothing if you think that is correct.

Fred: Hi, Ethel. I (see, *neg.*) _____ you _____ the end of last semester.
(1)   (2)

How (you/be) _____ all this time?
(3)

Ethel: Very busy, Fred. I (do) _____ a lot of work researching some major
(4)

changes in television.

Fred: Ah, yes. I think TV (change) _____ (fast) _____ of all the media.
(5)   (6)

Don't you agree?

Ethel: Absolutely, Fred. In your whole life, (see/you/ever) _____ so many
(7)

programs in so many different languages on TV? It's really amazing.

Fred: You're right; it *is* amazing. And it's great for improving your knowledge

in another language. With satellite dishes, you can get programs from

_____ Asia, _____ Middle East, _____ Europe, _____
(8)   (9)   (10)   (11)

Americas, and maybe from _____ Africa.
(12)

Ethel: Yeah, I have to say, of all the ways I (study) _____ new vocabulary
(13)

over the years, learning new words while listening to TV shows (be)

_____ (good) _____.
(14)   (15)

LEARNER LOG Check (✔) *Yes* or *I Need More Practice.*

Lesson	I Can Use . . .	Yes	I Need More Practice
26	The Zero Article and the Definite Article with Major Geographical Features		
27	The Present Perfect in Statements with *Be* and Other Verbs		
28	The Present Perfect in Questions and with the Words *Ever* and *Never*		
29	Regular and Irregular Superlative Adjectives and Adverbs		
30	Past, Present, and Future Tense		

APPENDIX 1	Activities for Student B

LESSON 2, PART 1, EXERCISE F (p. 14)
Student B looks at the text on this page. Student A looks at the text on page 14.
Ask questions to find the answers.

Sofonisba Anguissola was born in Italy. There were _____ (How many?) children in the family. Six of the children were daughters. _____ (Who?) was rich. Anguissola was an artist. She was very famous because she was _____ (Why?). Her sisters were artists too. In 1559, she went to Spain. She was a guest of _____ (Who?). She was very successful. Later in life she stopped painting because she was blind. She died in 1624. She was _____ (How old?) years old. Her paintings hang in many galleries in Europe.

LESSON 3, GRAMMAR AND VOCABULARY (p. 24)
Work with a classmate. Student B looks at the picture below. Student A looks at the picture on page 24. Describe what you both see in the picture. Find the six differences in the pictures. Use the grammar and vocabulary from the lesson.

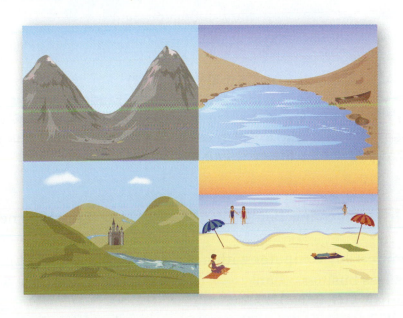

LESSON 4, PART 2, EXERCISE G (p. 33)

Student A turns to page 33. Student A asks Student B questions to complete the information about Basia. Student B asks Student A questions to complete the information about Panjit.

Basia

(who) FabriCare, Inc.
(what) seamstress
(where) Moscow, Russia
(how much) $5 per hour
(why) likes her coworkers

LESSON 8, GRAMMAR AND VOCABULARY (p. 62)

Work with a classmate. Student B looks at the picture below. Student A looks at the picture on page 62. Ask each other *yes/no* and information questions and answer the questions. Use vocabulary and grammar in this lesson.

LESSON 22, GRAMMAR AND VOCABULARY (p. 172)

Work with a classmate. Student B looks at this page. Student A looks at page 172. Student A reads the beginnings of the four conditional sentences to Student B. Student B chooses the best way to finish each sentence and tells Student A. Then reverse what you did for the next four sentences.

Student B:

1. a. if my Internet connection is okay.
   b. if my Internet connection is broken.

2. a. I may infect my computer with a virus.
   b. I shouldn't answer it.

3. a. it does less business than companies with one.
   b. it can have a website.

4. a. if they have internal e-mail.
   b. if they have the Internet.

5. If you aren't good in mathematics, . . .
6. Without a computer or fax machine, people . . .
7. People know more about other cultures now than ever before . . .
8. If a company needs to have a website, . . .

LESSON 23, PART 1, EXERCISE E (p. 177)

Work with a classmate. Imagine you are two actors. Student B looks at the information on this page. Student A looks at the information on page 177. Ask and answer questions to find the information. Use *be going to*.

Student B

In _____ : check on a patient

_____ : have quick lunch with her friends

Tonight: study at _____

_____ : go to yoga class

This fall: run a marathon with _____

_____ : ask for a pay raise

LESSON 28, PART 1, EXERCISE E (p. 215)

Work with a classmate. You are two actors waiting to have an audition with a director for a new movie. Student B, use the résumé below. Student A, use the résumé on page 215. Take turns asking about each other's experiences. Use the present perfect and simple past.

Student B

Movies
Love and Marriage (2002)
Big Hugs (2000)

TV
Laughs and Laughs (2002–present)
Comedy Hour (2000–2002)

Awards
Best New Comedy Actor, CelebrityNews.com (2003)

Education
Californian Film School – Film Studies Certificate (2005–present)
Drama School (2000–2002)

Student B Questions
1. be / in any movies?
2. be / in any TV shows?
3. How long / be / on *Years of Our Lives?*
4. win / any awards?
5. be / to drama school?
6. How long / be / film school?

■ **Adjective** An adjective describes a noun. Example: *That's a **small** desk.*

■ **Adverb** An adverb describes the verb of a sentence or an adjective. Examples: *He is **very** smart. I run **quickly**.*

■ **Adverb of Frequency** An adverb of frequency tells how often an action happens. Example: *I **always** go to the library after class.*

■ **Affirmative** An affirmative means *yes*.

■ **Apostrophe (')** See Appendix 8.

■ **Article** An article (*a, an,* and *the*) comes before a noun. Example: *I have **a** book and **an** eraser.*

■ **Base Form** The base form of a verb has no tense. It has no ending (*-s* or *-ed*). Examples: ***be, go, eat, take, write***

■ **Capitalization** See Appendix 7.

■ **Clause** A clause is a group of words that has a subject and a verb. Example: ***Harry likes** college.*

■ **Comma (,)** See Appendix 6.

■ **Comparative Form** A comparative form of an adjective or adverb is used to compare two things. Example: *I am **taller** than you.*

■ **Consonant** The following letters are consonants: ***b, c, d, f, g, h, j, k, l, m, n, p, q, r, s, t, v, w, x, y, z.***

■ **Contraction** A contraction is made up of two words put together with an apostrophe. Example: ***She's** my friend.* (She is = she's)

■ **Count Noun** Count nouns are nouns that we can count. They have a singular and a plural form. Examples: ***book – books, nurse – nurses***

■ **Frequency Expressions** Frequency expressions answer *How often* questions. Examples: ***once a week, three times a week, every day***

■ **Imperative** An imperative sentence gives a command or instructions. An imperative sentence usually omits the word *you*. Example: ***Open** the door.*

■ **Information Questions** Questions that ask *what, when, who, how,* or *which*.

■ **Irregular Verbs** See Appendix 4.

■ **Modal** Some examples of modal verbs are ***can, could, should, will, would, must**.*

■ **Negative** Means *no*.

■ **Noncount Noun** A noncount noun is a noun that we don't count. It has no plural form. Examples: ***water, money, rice***

■ **Noun** A noun is a word for a person, a place, or a thing. Nouns can be singular (only one) or plural (more than one).

■ **Object** The object of the sentence follows the verb. It receives the action of the verb. Example: *Kat wrote a **paragraph**.*

■ **Object Pronoun** Use object pronouns (*me, you, him, her, it, us, them*) after the verb or preposition. Example: *Kat wore **it**.*

■ **Period (.)** See Appendix 8.

- **Plural** Plural means more than one. A plural noun usually ends with -s or -es. Examples: *The books are heavy. The buses are not running.*

- **Possessive Form** The possessive form of a noun has an apostrophe: *the teacher's class, Jupiter's moons.* Possessive pronouns *(my, mine, our, ours, his, her, hers, their, theirs, its, your, yours)* do not use an apostrophe.

- **Preposition** A preposition is a short, connecting word. Examples: *about, above, across, after, around, as, at, away, before, behind, below, by, down, for, from, in, into, like, of, on, out, over, to, under, up, with*

- **Punctuation (. , ' ?)** Punctuation marks are used to make writing clear (for example: periods, commas, apostrophes, question marks). See Appendix 8.

- **Question Mark (?)** See Appendix 8.

- **Regular Verb** A regular verb forms its past tense with -d or -ed. Example: *He lived in Mexico.*

- **Sentence** A sentence is a group of words that contains a subject and a verb and expresses a complete thought.

- **Singular** Means one.

- **Stative Verb** Stative verbs have no action. They do not often take the progressive form. Examples: *love, like, think, own, understand, want*

- **Subject** The subject of the sentence tells who or what the sentence is about. Example: *The **water** does not taste good.*

- **Subject Pronoun** Use subject pronouns *(I, you, he, she, it, we, they)* in place of a subject noun. Example: ***They*** (= *the books*) *are on the desk.*

- **Tense** A verb has tense. Tense shows when the action of the sentence happened.

    Simple Present: *She occasionally **reads** before bed.*

    Present Progressive: *He **is thinking** about it now.*

    Simple Past: *I **talked** to him yesterday.*

- **Verb** Verbs are words of action or state. Example: *I **go** to work every day. Joe **stays** at home.*

- **Yes/No Questions** Yes/No questions ask for a *yes* or *no* answer. Example: *Is she from Mexico? **Yes,** she is.*

The irregular verbs in each box contain the same sound change from the basic form (on the left) to the simple past (on the right). You will need to memorize the verbs in each box.

come	came
become	became

drink	drank
ring	rang
sing	sang

lend	lent
send	sent
spend	spent

drive	drove
ride	rode
write	wrote

bite	bit
hide	hid

shake	shook
take	took

speak	spoke
steal	stole

cost	cost
cut	cut
hit	hit
hurt	hurt
put	put
quit	quit
shut	shut

get	got
forget	forgot

blow	blew
draw	drew
fly	flew
grow	grew
know	knew
throw	threw

feed	fed
feel	felt
keep	kept
leave	left
lead	led
meet	met
read	read*
sleep	slept

* Pronounced "red"

sell	sold
tell	told

begin	began
sit	sat
swim	swam

bring	brought
buy	bought
catch	caught*
fight	fought
teach	taught*
think	thought

* The spelling is different for these two verbs: -au- not -ou-

stand	stood
understand	understood

break	broke
tear	tore
wake	woke
wear	wore

The following chart gives the past and past participles of some common verbs. You must memorize these forms, because they are irregular.

Base Form	Past Tense	Past Participle
be	was, were	been
begin	began	begun
bite	bit	bitten
break	broke	broken
bring	brought	brought
build	built	built
buy	bought	bought
catch	caught	caught
choose	chose	chosen
come	came	come
cost	cost	cost
cut	cut	cut
do	did	done
draw	drew	drawn
drink	drank	drunk
eat	ate	eaten
feel	felt	felt
find	found	found
give	gave	given
go	went	gone
grow	grew	grown
hide	hid	hidden
have	had	had
hear	heard	heard
keep	kept	kept
know	knew	known
make	made	made
pay	paid	paid
read	read	read
say	said	said
see	saw	seen
speak	spoke	spoken
take	took	taken
teach	taught	taught
tell	told	told
think	thought	thought
write	wrote	written

Study the verb charts below. They show how verbs are conjugated in the present, past, progressive, perfect, and future tenses.

The Present and Past of *Be:* Statements

Subject	*Be*		Subject	*Be*	
I	am	a teacher.	I	was	a doctor.
	am not			was not	
He	is		He	was	
She	is not	warm.	She	was not	warm yesterday.
It			It		
We	are		We	were	
You	are not	Mexicans.	You	were not	in Mexico last year.
They			They		

See Lesson 1.

Simple Present Tense: Statements

Affirmative Statements			**Negative Statements**			
Subject	Verb		Subject	*Do Not*	Verb	
I			I			
You	work	in South Korea.	You	do not	work	in Japan.
We			We	don't		
They			They			
He			He			
She	comes	from Mexico.	She	does not	come	from Peru.
It			It	doesn't		

See Lesson 4.

Present Progressive: Affirmative and Negative Statements

Affirmative Statements

Subject	*Be*	Verb + *-ing*
I	am	**reading** about Sedna.
He She It	is	**orbiting** Earth.
You We They	are	**studying** astronomy.

Negative Statements

Subject	*Be + Not*	Verb + *-ing*
I	am not	**reading** about Mars.
He She It	is not	**orbiting** the moon.
You We They	are not	**studying** biology.

See Lesson 8.

The Simple Past Tense Affirmative Statements

Subject	Base Form of Verb + *-d/-ed*	
I You He She It We They	**arrived**	yesterday. in 1984. a year ago.

The Simple Past Tense Negative Statements

Subject	*did + not*	Base Form of Verb	
I You He She It We They	**did not** (OR) **didn't**	**arrive**	last week. this morning. a month ago.

See Lesson 16.

The Simple Past Tense Affirmative Statements

Subject	Past Form of Verb	
I You He She It We They	**made**	a discovery.

The Simple Past Tense Negative Statements

Subject	*Did + Not*	Base Form of Verb	
I You He She It We They	**did not** (OR) **didn't**	**make**	a discovery.

See Lesson 17.

The Past Progressive: Statements

Subject	*Be* in the Past	Verb + *-ing*	
I He She	was was not		
You We They	were were not	looking	for fossils last week.

See Lesson 18.

Be Going To in Statements

Subject	*Be Going To*	Verb	
I	am going to am not going to	be	a licensed practical nurse.
He She	is going to isn't going to	have	clinical classes in a hospital.
We You They	are going to aren't going to	take	one year to finish the program.
It	is going to	rain.	

See Lesson 23.

Will in Statements

Subject	*Will* + Base Verb	
I He They	will live won't live	on Mars one day.

See Lesson 24.

The Present Perfect: Affirmative Statements with *For* and *Since*

Subject	*Have*	Been Participle		*For* or *Since*
I	have			for a long time.
You	have not			for six months.
We	haven't	been	married	for five minutes.
They				
She	has			since 1995.
He	hasn't			since last year.

See Lesson 27.

The Present Perfect: *Yes/No* Questions and Short Answers

Have	Subject	Past Participle		Short Answers
Have	you			Yes, I have.
		seen	the movie?	No, I haven't.
Has	she			Yes, she has.
				No, she hasn't.

See Lesson 28.

Do vs. Make

When you *do* something, there is an activity, some kind of action. When you *make* something, you create something that did not exist before.
You do exercises, the laundry / dishes (= wash), homework, gardening, a job, what's right, etc.
You make a telephone call, a reservation, a cake, an appointment, plans, a decision, etc.

Hear vs. Listen To

When there is a sound or noise, you *hear* it. You have no control over this. This is what your ears do. We call this an involuntary action. When you pay attention to a sound or noise, you *listen to* it.
Be quiet for a moment. I think I hear somebody outside. Who could it be?
I have to give a short speech in class tomorrow. Can you please listen to me while I practice it?

Say vs. Tell

When we use the verb *say,* we normally don't mention the person who is listening. When we use the verb *tell,* we must mention the person who is listening. With *tell,* we can also use the infinitive verb.
She said (that) we needed to pay in cash.
She told <u>us</u> (that) we needed to pay in cash. / She told <u>us</u> to pay in cash.

See vs. Look At vs. Watch

When you open your eyes, you *see.* You have no control over this. This is another involuntary action. When you pay attention to something that is not doing an activity, you *look at* it. When you pay attention to something that is doing an activity, you *watch* it. *Look at* and *watch* are more examples of voluntary actions.
Jim doesn't see well. That's why he wears glasses.
Look at that sunset! I never saw the sun with such a deep orange color.
I like to watch my dogs play with each other in the backyard.
The one exception is *to see a movie.* (You *watch* a television show.)

Talk vs. Speak

These verbs have the same meaning ("have a conversation"), but you *talk to* somebody or you *speak to / with* somebody. The only big difference is that you *speak* a language, not *talk.*
Can I talk to you for a minute, Mr. Conklin? / Can I speak to / with you for a minute, Mr. Conklin?
He's amazing. He can speak six languages.

Capitalize:

- the first word in a sentence. Example: *The college is closed today.*
- names and titles. Examples: *Manuel, Mrs. Jones, President Johnson*
- geographic names. Examples: *Brazil, Paris, Federal Street, the Atlantic Ocean*
- names of organizations and businesses. Examples: *Boston University, United Nations, Thomson Heinle*
- days of the week, months, and holidays. Examples: *Monday, July, Christmas*
- nationalities, languages, religions, and ethnic groups. Examples: *Russians, English, Islam, Hispanics*
- main words in book and movie titles. Examples: *Grammar Connection, Gone with the Wind*

- Use an **apostrophe** ('):
  1. to show possession. Example: *That is Ivan's pen.*
  2. for contractions. Example: *I didn't (= did not) go to class yesterday.*
- Use a **comma** (,):
  1. in a list of two or more things. Example: *I have class on Monday, Wednesday, and Friday.*
  2. in answers with *yes* or *no*. Examples: *Yes, I do. No, I don't feel well.*
  3. in statements or questions with *and, but,* or *so*. Examples: *My sister is a student, and she is studying engineering. Kobe is good at math, but Simone is good at art.*
- Use an **exclamation mark** (!) to express surprise, shock, or delight. Example: *Oh no! I forgot my homework!*
- Use a **period** (.):
  1. at the end of a sentence. Example: *Francis goes to Hedden Community College.*
  2. after many common abbreviations. Examples: *Mr., Mrs., Dr., Ave.*
- Use a **question mark** (?) at the end of a question. Example: *Do you study math?*

Cardinal Numbers

1	one
2	two
3	three
4	four
5	five
6	six
7	seven
8	eight
9	nine
10	ten
11	eleven
12	twelve
13	thirteen
14	fourteen
15	fifteen
16	sixteen
17	seventeen
18	eighteen
19	nineteen
20	twenty
21	twenty-one
30	thirty
40	forty
50	fifty
60	sixty
70	seventy
80	eighty
90	ninety
100	one hundred
1,000	one thousand
10,000	ten thousand
100,000	one hundred thousand
1,000,000	one million

Ordinal Numbers

first	1st
second	2nd
third	3rd
fourth	4th
fifth	5th
sixth	6th
seventh	7th
eighth	8th
ninth	9th
tenth	10th
eleventh	11th
twelfth	12th
thirteenth	13th
fourteenth	14th
fifteenth	15th
sixteenth	16th
seventeenth	17th
eighteenth	18th
nineteenth	19th
twentieth	20th
twenty-first	21st

Days of the Week

Sunday
Monday
Tuesday
Wednesday
Thursday
Friday
Saturday

Seasons

winter
spring
summer
fall/autumn

Months of the Year

January
February
March
April
May
June
July
August
September
October
November
December

Write the Date

April 5, 2004 = 4/5/04

Temperature Chart

Degrees Celsius (°C) and
Degrees Fahrenheit (°F)

100°C	212°F
30°C	86°F
25°C	77°F
20°C	68°F
15°C	59°F
10°C	50°F
5°C	41°F
0°C	32°F
−5°C	23°F

Weights and Measures

Weight:

1 pound (lb.) = 453.6 grams (g)
16 ounces (oz.) = 1 pound (lb.)
1 pound (lb.) = .45 kilograms (kg)

Liquid or Volume:

1 cup (c.) = .24 liter (l)
2 cups (c.) = 1 pint (pt.)
2 pints = 1 quart (qt.)
4 quarts = 1 gallon (gal.)
1 gallon (gal.) = 3.78 liters (l)

Length:

1 inch (in. or ") = 2.54 centimeters (cm)
1 foot (ft. or ') = .3048 meters (m)
12 inches (12") = 1 foot (1')
1 yard (yd.) = 3 feet (3') or 0.9144 meters (m)
1 mile (mi.) = 1,609.34 meters (m) or 1.609 kilometers (km)

Time:

60 seconds = 1 minute
60 minutes = 1 hour
24 hours = 1 day
28–31 days = 1 month
12 months = 1 year

Review: Lessons 1–5
(pages 41–42)

A.

1. 's/is
2. How is
3. I'm
4. it's/it is
5. Do
6. in
7. far
8. from
9. There's/There is
10. Does
11. is
12. in
13. for
14. take
15. on
16. have
17. on
18. starts
19. at
20. ends
21. at
22. is
23. from
24. until
25. go
26. after
27. is
28. 's/is
29. There were
30. in
31. there are
32. come
33. from
34. Some/a few
35. in
36. before
37. At
38. after
39. walk
40. around

B.

1. is
2. was
3. is
4. There are
5. in
6. What
7. are
8. at
9. What
10. is
11. need
12. some/a few
13. aren't
14. don't understand
15. want
16. don't have
17. Does
18. Which
19. gives
20. How long
21. is
22. Does
23. where
24. is
25. Is
26. near

Review: Lessons 6–10
(pages 79–80)

A.

1. First
2. in
3. Next/Then
4. in
5. Next/Then
6. out of
7. on
8. in
9. Then
10. in
11. Next/Then
12. Next/Then
13. by
14. in

B.

1. do these books and this book bag belong
2. they
3. yours
4. they
5. mine
6. They
7. Ben's
8. Does Ben have
9. don't think
10. his
11. I
12. it
13. it
14. belongs
15. Jessica's
16. mine
17. We
18. own
19. She
20. owns
21. one
22. one
23. mine
24. They
25. my
26. brother's
27. them
28. He
29. they

C.

1. are you going
2. feel
3. want
4. are you asking
5. Do you want
6. don't like
7. tastes
8. smells
9. think
10. bring
11. didn't bring

12. 'm not living
13. Are you having
14. is painting
15. is talking

Review: Lessons 11–15 (pages 115–116)

A.
1. –
2. smarter than
3. –
4. The
5. as
6. as
7. a
8. –
9. A
10. same
11. –
12. A
13. different
14. –
15. smarter
16. –
17. better
18. than
19. –
20. –
21. worse than
22. a
23. a
24. the
25. more
26. fewer
27. than
28. A
29. easier
30. cuter
31. more interesting than
32. a

B.
1. less
2. hard
3. carefully
4. much/a lot of
5. fast
6. slowly

7. right
8. correctly
9. too few
10. more efficiently
11. more
12. better
13. less
14. more
15. less
16. less
17. a little
18. a lot of

Review: Lessons 16–20 (pages 157–158)

A.
1. Did
2. barbecue
3. when
4. lived
5. did
6. did
7. choose
8. put
9. put
10. ago
11. when
12. had
13. started
14. burned
15. Before
16. didn't have
17. after
18. passed
19. shouldn't

B.
1. When
2. was buying
3. found
4. when
5. took
6. began
7. shouldn't
8. before
9. Did
10. take
11. before

12. tried
13. did
14. should be
15. did
16. happen
17. were
18. doing
19. when
20. was
21. moving
22. Did
23. bite
24. when
25. moved
26. don't have to worry

Review: Lessons 21–25 (pages 197–198)

A.
1. Could
2. If
3. 'll tell
4. may
5. 're having
6. would like
7. if
8. is
9. will
10. be
11. could be
12. may/might/could have
13. if
14. have
15. 'll have
16. If
17. brings
18. will
19. will
20. If
21. reserve
22. offer
23. there are
24. 'll give

B.
1. Could
2. If
3. will
4. 'd

5. won't look
6. if
7. did
8. 'm going to be/'ll be
9. want
10. 'd like
11. will give
12. If
13. won't quit
14. I'm

Review: Lessons 26–30
(pages 233–234)

A.

1. the
2. –
3. the
4. Have you ever been
5. I haven't
6. 've never been
7. the
8. farthest
9. have changed
10. since
11. the
12. the most beautiful
13. the most relaxing
14. the
15. –
16. the
17. the loveliest
18. the calmest
19. 've ever visited
20. the
21. –
22. the nicest
23. the kindest
24. the
25. the friendliest
26. –
27. the
28. Has it been
29. for
30. hasn't been
31. since
32. –
33. the fastest
34. began
35. have visited
36. the

B.

1. haven't seen
2. since
3. have you been
4. 've been doing
5. changes
6. the fastest
7. have you ever seen
8. –
9. the
10. –
11. the
12. –
13. 've studied
14. was
15. the best

Words in blue are part of the Content Vocabulary section at the start of each lesson.
Words in black are words glossed with the readings in each lesson.
Words in **bold** are words from the Academic Word List.

Illustrators

Richard Carbajal/illustrationOnLine.com: pp. 3, 20, 167, 181–182, 185–186.

Amy Cartwright/illustrationOnLine.com: pp. 24, 49, 63, 65 (top), 66, 69, 95, 98, 100, 102, 189, 192, 195, 235.

InContext Publishing Partners: pp. 131, 149 (middle), 231.

Alan King/illustrationOnLine.com: pp. 55, 58, 60–62, 81, 87, 92–93 (top), 205, 211, 225, 236.

Katie McCormick/illustrationOnLine.com: pp. 43, 71, 75, 76–77, 103, 105, 125, 133, 159, 173, 176–177 (top 2 illustrations).

Precision Graphics: pp. 8–9, 11, 13, 19 (bottom), 21–23, 37, 41–42, 48, 65 (bottom), 70, 85, 89, 93 (bottom), 109, 111–114, 138 (bottom), 141, 143 (far left), 175, 177 (bottom), 179, 183, 187, 203–204, 207, 210, 215, 219, 229, 237.

David Preiss/Munro Campagna.com: pp. 1, 17–18, 19 (top), 135–136, 138 (top), 142.

Scott Wakefield/Gwen Walters Artist Representative: pp. 25, 27, 35, 117, 120–121.

Philip Williams/illustrationOnLine.com: pp. 143 (middle and right), 147–148, 149 (left and right).

Photo Credits